Published by:
McNeil Consulting Inc.
108 Nottingham Drive
Spring City, PA 19475

Printed in the USA
Version 2.2 February 2019

Moving Experiences: Advanced Facilitation Laboratory Handbook. The authors reserve all rights, including, without limitation, all rights under the US and International copyright and trademark laws. No part of this publication may be reproduced, stored in a retrieval system, or transmitted in any form or media by any means, electronic, mechanical, photocopying, recording, or otherwise, without the prior written permission of the authors. This copyrighted publication may not be resold, relicensed, exported, redistributed, otherwise transferred, or used in any manner by any party other than the person or entity to whom it is sold for use. Any violation of these restrictions may infringe upon the authors' copyright under 17 USC 106(3), and any such violation shall automatically terminate the right to use this publication.

AUTHORS	3
INTRODUCTION	4
5 DAY LABORATORY SCHEDULE	5
INTRODUCTION TO THE DESIGNS	7
BRIEF SYNOPSIS OF THE DESIGNS	8
MY 13 MAXIMS	10
DAY 1- GETTING STARTED	14
1. INTRODUCING EACH OTHER	14
2. WARM-UP EXERCISES	16
3. LIFE STORIES	18
4. HORSE TRADING	23
5. COUNT TO TWENTY	25
6. GROUP DYNAMICS	27
DAY 2 - ACTION RESEARCH	31
7. REFLECTIONS	31
WHAT IS ACTION RESEARCH?	32
8. SINGING OUR SONGS	34
9. FAIRY TALES	37
10. GROUP JUGGLING	39
11. REAL-TIME INTERVIEWS	42
12. ROTATIONAL ACTION PLANNING	48
DAY 3 – INNOVATION THEME	51
13. THE IMPACT WHEEL	51
14. DIGITAL DECISION-MAKING	54

15. THE VIRTUAL HIVE	57
16. CONCORDANT DECISION-MAKING	59
17. THE EXECUTIVE HERE AND NOW	61
18. COVER STORY	62
DAY 4 - TEAMS AND THE MATRIX	64
19. DREXLER SIBBET TEAM ASSESSMENT	64
20. VALENTINES	68
21. TWO TRUTHS AND A LIE	70
22. THE PRISONER'S DILEMMA	71
23. RENEW AND RESTORE	74
DAY FIVE - FEEDBACK AND CLOSE	77
24. THE DESIGN CLINIC	77
25. GENIE IN THE BOTTLE	79
26. THE YOGI CLOSE	81
GROUP DYNAMICS - GROUP OBSERVATION FORM	86
GROUP DYNAMICS - WHO TALKS TO WHOM FORM	87
PRISONER'S DILEMMA - INSTRUCTION SHEET	88
PRISONER'S DILEMMA - PAYOFF SCHEDULE	89
YOGI BERRA QUOTES	90
REAL-TIME INTERVIEW SESSION AND ROOM SET-UP	92

Authors

Robert and Christine McNeil

Company website: http://www.robertmcneil.com
Phone: 610 331-4187
Email: rob@robertmcneil.com
Address: 108 Nottingham Drive, Spring City, PA 19475

Rob McNeil is the President and founder of McNeil Consulting Inc., and has worked in the field of management consulting since 1980. He works with organizations large and small, global, and local. The company helps organizations lead successful change efforts, build high-performing teams, align their business strategy, and develop their leaders in service of their customers.

He created the company in 1987 based on the work of his teachers, Alan Drexler, Marv Weisbord, Elsie Y. Cross, and Will Schutz. McNeil Consulting Inc. creates real value by helping our clients to increase engagement, build trust, improve productivity, and elevate their customer experience.

Christine McNeil has an extensive public service-background with a concentration on local, regional, and federal planning, grants administration, and fund raising. She brings together diverse clients to build teams, create strategic plans, and gain consensus. She has led large, multiple-year regional strategic planning initiatives. The Schutz Company, Designed Learning, and Drexler Sibbet certify Chris in Life Orientations, Staff Consulting Skills, and Team Performance Systems. She is Vice President of McNeil Consulting Inc., and resides in northern Chester County, PA where she has served for 10 years as an elected local township supervisor and the Vice Chairwoman of two regional planning committees.

Introduction

Kurt Lewin is famous for saying, "There is nothing so practical as a good theory." It follows that a few good theories offer unique perspectives on group life and offer us a terrific way to think about the concept of "design" in terms of our meetings. Our workshop is based on three theories of group development. These are the theories and models we use:

The Drexler Sibbet Team Performance Model features the journey the team takes though time on its way to high performance. It is unique in that the graphic format creates a map, a lexicon, and a process in one picture. The seven lenses also offer a way to look inside the model at the keys to each stage. We use this model to help our clients develop a language to talk about team development. You will also see in this workshop that the model offers a means to design meetings and strategic off-sites by assessing what a team needs to explore to further its own development.

Will Schutz developed the FIRO model (later called The Human Element), which stands for Fundamental Interpersonal Relations Orientation. Will believed understanding this model is essential in terms of interpersonal relationships. The needs he observed are: Inclusion, Control, and Openness. When we design, we keep these foremost in our minds.

Yvonne Agassarian created the Living System Theory of Groups and illustrated them as living systems. Her writing is amazingly clear about how groups form and work. She illuminated how important it is to identify the sub-teams (sub groups) within any group as a means of understanding the dynamics that underlie performance. Optimizing sub groups is a terrific way to create the possibility for extraordinary team performance.

Google spent fifty million dollars researching team development. They studied 180 teams and took two years to complete their work. Known as **the Aristotle Project**, this research provided support for all the above theories. We urge you to read the research as a way to develop your own personal approach to facilitation, teamwork, and organizational development. Much of what is included in this workshop is supported by their findings.

5 Day Laboratory Schedule

Day 1 - Getting Started
Morning Session
- Welcome
- Introductions (*Inclusion*)
- Introducing Yourself
- Action Research Facilitation and My 13 Maxims
- Theories of Group Development
- Expectations
- How the workshop unfolds
- Choice
- Your involvement is requested. Everything is voluntary (*Control*)
- Request volunteers to lead Your next Exercise
- Behavioral Imagery
- Getting to Know You
- Life Stories (*Openness*)
- How to Process an Experience
- Giving and Receiving Feedback
- Horse Trading
- Who does what from this point on? (*Control*)

Afternoon Session
- Warm up
- Count to Twenty
- The Group Dynamics Exercise
- Observations and Debriefing Experiences
- Horse Trading
- Choosing the experience, you want to facilitate
- Homework time

Day 2 - Action Research
Morning Session
- Check-in and Reflections
- Defining Action Research
- Creative Diagnostics
- Singing Our Songs
- Fairy Tales

Afternoon Session
- Group Juggling
- Real-time Interviews
- Rotational Action Planning

Day 3 - Innovation
Morning Session
- Reflections
- The Impact Wheel
- Digital Decision-Making
- The Virtual Hive

Afternoon Session
- Warm-up Exercise
- Concordant Decision-making
- Executive Here and Now Session
- Cover Story

Day 4 - Teams and the Matrix
Morning Session
- Reflections
- Assessing Teams with the Drexler Sibbet Model
- Contracting and delivering a Team off-site
- Valentines

Afternoon Session
- Warm-up
- Two Truths and a Lie
- The Prisoner's Dilemma
- Renew and Restore

Day 5 - Feedback and Closing
Morning Session
- Reflections
- Genie in the Bottle
- The Design Clinic
- Yogi Close
- Next Steps

Introduction to the Designs

The Advanced Facilitation Laboratory is a workshop and workbook that contains 26 Great Designs. When we say "design," we mean a series of visual and interactive activities that require your participation. You will be learning these designs by leading them and facilitating the discussions that follow the design. Each member of your workshop will be responsible for taking a particular design from start to finish. For this workshop, you will be working mostly in teams of two.

One of our first activities will be to choose the design you want to lead and facilitate, and the teammates who will work with you. We will be setting this up at the end of our first day together. To help you decide which design you would like to facilitate, please look at the designs in this book and their descriptions. Think about one that might stretch your skills, one that interests you, or one that you might use in an upcoming meeting. You will be taking part in all of them, so you are only choosing the one you think you want to lead / facilitate.

The experiences are presented in five categories:
- Opening and Getting Started
- Action Research
- Innovation
- Teams and the Matrix
- Feedback and Closing

The opening and group dynamic designs take place on the first day.
The second day focuses on data collection and presentation.
The third day focuses on innovation and problem solving.
The fourth day is focused on creating your own designs and resolving conflict.
The final day is devoted to personal feedback and closing the workshop.

Brief Synopsis of the Designs

When teaching the workshop as a multi-day event, post each design with the names of the facilitators on large sticky notes. If you do have to re-arrange your schedule, this will make it easier for you and the group to do so.

Day 1 - Getting Started

Introducing Yourself is a wonderful way for the group to get to know each other.
Behavioral Imagery illustrates FIRO theory. It is another way to look at groups and teams.
Life Stories is all about disclosure, feedback, and connections.
Horse Trading is a wonderful way to involve everyone in the workshop.
Count to Twenty is a fun warm-up to discover how to create a very close sense of group unity.
The Group Dynamics Exercise reviews group process and illustrates all the group theories presented in the workshop. Participants often describe it as an entire semester of a masters-level group dynamics course.

Day 2 - Action Research

The Checking In and Reflections Processes are important ways to begin meetings. This is a simple practice session using our own experience.
Singing Our Songs is a data collection exercise. It is an eye-opening experience for what is possible with teams.
Fairy Tales is a unique organizational assessment. It is a classic favorite for our participants.
Group Juggling may appear to be a simple warm-up, but it can also be used to talk about project teams and continuous improvement.
Real-time Interviews is used to take an organizational assessment. It has many uses that can be applied in many different situations. It is an alternative to surveys for collecting critical information and working it in real-time.
Rotational Action Planning can have a key place in strategic off-sites where the goal is to create buy-in as part of the planning process. It saves time and is another consensus-building activity.

Day 3 - Innovation and Decision-Making

The Impact Wheel is a fun exercise that helps groups see past the default scenarios for what they think might happen. It is highly involving and illustrates creative thinking in groups.
Digital Decision-Making is a very structured approach to help groups lay out the core elements that go into making their decision. It is useful to help teams to move forward when they are stuck on a decision.

The Virtual Hive revolutionizes manual facilitation. Consider making use of Groupware to take facilitation to a whole new level.

Concordant Decision Making is one step beyond consensus. It makes full use of inclusion, control, and openness.

The Executive Here and Now Session is designed as a trust-building exercise for teams. It is an enormously powerful tool to have in your quiver.

Cover Story is an innovative way to investigate the future. It is highly motivating and up lifting and is an effective way to help a group see new ideas about what is possible.

Day 4 - Teams and the Matrix

The Drexler Sibbet Team Assessment will allow you to help teams to do an informal assessment of their progress towards high performance.

Valentines is a feedback-rich design for working with sub-teams within large groups or different teams that have to work together. It is sometimes called "the team-to-team exercise."

Two Truths and a Lie is a classic game that is great as a conversation starter. It encourages team members to disclose relevant information to other team members.

The Prisoner's Dilemma comes from game theory. This design is not meant for team building but it can be illuminating as a metaphor for working in the matrix organization.

Renew and Restore helps many executives renew and or restore their relationships with other executives with whom they have had interpersonal difficulties.

Day 5 - Feedback and Closings

Genie in the Bottle is pure action research applied to giving and receiving feedback. It is wonderful way to review all we have learned this week.

The Design Clinic features small group sharing and each participant presents an upcoming meeting, or consulting engagement that they would like help to design.

The Yogi Close shows us that endings can be fun, powerful, and memorable. Enjoy this one and use it with your own teams. Yogi deserves to be remembered by us all.

My 13 Maxims

Summary

The Maxims are conversation starters that help to ease the participants into the session. The Maxims are short statements that I believe to be true about group theory and its application to the real world. We decided to find a way to start engaging conversations about interesting topics that related directly to group dynamics and facilitation. The response to the Maxims has been universally positive. Participants often will chime in with their own examples of how several Maxims have played out for them.

They want you to succeed.

Whenever you start a meeting, begin a talk, or open a workshop, the group creates a positive and safe place for you. This space is always present at the beginning and you can count on it being there for you. Groups want to have a valuable experience, a meaningful event, and a memorable day. They are rooting for you. They want you to succeed. So, enjoy this space, take this special opportunity to give the group a positive experience and meet them with a warm welcome and invite them to the work. Your first job is to be inclusive and welcoming. If your beginning is both invitational and voluntary, you can be rest assured that your beginning design will work.

Minimum effort for maximum effect.

Designs are created to help the group to do its work. Keep your designs as simple as possible and your instructions as short and as clear as you can. Get out of the group's way and allow them to maximize their effort and to (ultimately) do own their work. One of the skill sets needed of a great facilitator is to step back and let go of the design. Someone once described what we do as "wind them up and let them go." In this book you will find very clear instructions on how to set up the mechanics for each design. Sometimes the hardest part is to let the design do what it is supposed to do, and not interfere with the group as it goes about its work.

Never work harder than your client.

Clients will do all sorts of things to get you to be involved in their work to a greater extent than you need to be. Never forget this. Most of us got into this line of work because we like people, and we also like to be liked. Wanting to be liked can morph into being more helpful than what is called for. One of my teachers once said, "Don't just do something, stand there." It turned out to be great advice. The group's work is their work. It is not our work. It is best not to tie ourselves to outcomes we think the group wants. As a facilitator, you also need to be aware that there is a tendency for the group to flee the work, especially when it starts to become ambiguous, risky, difficult, and messy. Remember that groups either work or they flee. It is instinctual. And if they want to flee, they will likely look to you for help. You cannot want their outcome more than they do.

98 percent of consulting mistakes come from contracting.
You really cannot facilitate until you have a clear working contract of what the client wants and what you will deliver. Contracting works backwards from the outcomes. What the client wants I make sure I can deliver. And then I also make sure that I ask for what I need and follow up so that the client delivers what I need. In our work it is important to remember Robert Frost's line, "Good fences make good neighbors." Often, clear boundaries determine the quality of the work done.

One thing we have learned over the years is that we can always re-contract. For example, if we have a feeling the client is not following through on their part, we can call for a re-contracting session to clear things up and to get both of us on the same page. Misunderstanding often comes from good intent. Learning how and when to call for a re-contracting session is critical to meeting the clients' wants while satisfying my own, as well.

Design, then edit.
For new facilitators, there is a tendency to over-design. Clients will also want to include more activities into a design than it can hold. Believe this and expect them to do it. We see this all the time in our advanced facilitation design workshops. The ability to edit well is the mark of a seasoned facilitator. Group work always takes more time than estimated. Discussions will go on for longer than expected, key people will return late from breaks, and nervous presenters will demand more time to get their thoughts in order. Plan for all of these in your design and then be strong about editing. Sometimes editing means adding something in, but from my experience this is usually quite rare.

Conflict requires deep entry first.
Often, our best work leads to healthy and productive conflict. When you sense conflict, you must enter deeply into it. I learned this from George Leonard, the great author and one of my Aikido instructors. By entering deep, I mean working to create a safe place and directing the group to enter with you. Deep implies very focused listening combined with openness. We must model for the group the courage to ask what no one else will. Ask what the silence means. Ask why the woman who last spoke was simply left hanging. Take the risk to support those who are afraid to speak up. Simply be curious as to what is happening and stay present. Most times, when conflict arises in groups, they have not had a good history working with it. This is where you can add the most value.

A group will not go any further than it will go.
I have learned that groups set their own boundaries. My job is to push them to their limit and no more. We can ask group members to take the risk that needs taking, knowing that the work is voluntary and ultimately driven by the choices they make. Group members must learn to recognize the power of choice in group

life. When group members feel invited, understand that their participation is voluntary, and collectively get to decide on their agenda and their priorities, real accountability occurs. As facilitators, we do not have to push the group to where we think it should go. They already know.

Leverage feedback.
Feedback is an acquired taste. Performance improvement requires two things: focused practice and real-time feedback. Ask any great athlete, musician, or speaker. They will tell you the same. I believe my job, as a facilitator is to provide by design as many ways as possible for leaders and their teams to create their own feedback loops. This does not mean they always like it, especially in the beginning. It takes a while to get the hang of asking for feedback and then being free to give it. Feedback itself requires focused practice. Our intention needs to align with our actions, and we must get the courage to say what we see. Receiving feedback also requires focused practice. Really hearing feedback and taking it all in is an amazing experience for most teams. Once they get it, they will want to become more data driven and more experiential in their approach to their work.

Ask the group.
One of the most embarrassing things we often see is a leader who loses the group. It usually looks like the following: the leader is showing a PowerPoint and does not realize that they no longer have the group interested in what they are saying. At some point, the leader realizes that they have lost the group, but they have no idea of what to do next. So, what they do is either double down on the presentation or start to move more quickly through the slides, speeding up the presentation and trying to put an end to a painful experience. Both solutions are ineffective.

What the leader needs to do is to stop presenting and ask the group for help. They could say, "I am picking up that I have lost your interest. Please help me out. Can anyone explain where I got off track?" In my experience the group will always jump to the leader's aid. The reason is the same as for the grace period above. The team is rooting for you and wants to help. They want you to give a great presentation. This intervention always works if the leader waits for an answer. It may take a few painful seconds before someone speaks up. Once someone speaks, others will speak. Chart their thoughts and then continue with the presentation. They will appreciate getting involved, and the leader, because of the vulnerability they displayed, goes up in the eyes of the group. It is simple but not easy. This maxim also applies to any and all interventions you may make as a group facilitator. If you are wrong, the group will tell you. Isn't that wonderful?

Equalize the risk.
If you want to help teams create safety, show them how important it is to equalize the risk for saying what needs to be said to the team. Start small. Ask people to

share something about themselves that others may not know. Ask that everyone share. When giving feedback, make sure that everyone gets involved in giving and receiving. The general rule to follow is that each of us has part of the truth, and we need to hear from everyone to understand the whole. My organic chemistry professor drilled into me his most important law, Baldy's Law: "Some of it, plus the rest of it, equals all of it." Stated in group terms, if I know that I will be at the same level of risk as everyone else, I am more likely to relax, cut you some slack, and open up to the group.

Group issues do not resolve on their own.
The unwelcome news is that negative group issues do not resolve. The good news is that they continue to repeat until they get resolved. The other good news is that a facilitator can be helpful to a group with negative issues. You can help raise the issues that need to be discussed. You can help create a safe place to discuss those issues. You can also design effective processes for resolving issues as a normal part of the team's work. Groups can rarely resolve their negative issues on their own. They are too close to them, and these negative issues are reinforced by the norms the group lives by. Groups also do not have the language to speak about what is going on or a model to help them gain perspective. This is where we as facilitators can add real value.

Build healthy norms.
Did you ever wonder why facilitators split teams into smaller groups? "It's so that everyone gets more air time." "More intimate conversations can occur as team members feel safer." "It's easier to listen, and easier to be understood." All are true and yet there is also another especially important reason: groups form norms. These are undiscussed ways of interacting. The power of the norms is that they are agreed to by everyone. A facilitator helps teams to create powerful norms of relating to each other. Manage the norms and you do not need to worry about the individuals. Here is the secret: the norms teams create in small groups tend to carry over to the large group! So, the more that the teammates create good norms in the small groups, the easier it is for them to work well in the large team.

Be here now.
Group work can be divided into "here and now," and "there and then." Whenever teams become frightened or bored, they tend to move into there and then. Your job as a facilitator is to encourage the team to stay here and now. It is not easy, as you will become frightened and bored as well. Good comments to use in such circumstances are: "What's happening right now?" or "What just happened?" Be prepared to say what you are seeing and feeling. Ask first, and then give your thoughts and feelings. Great designs focus on sequencing here and now experiences. They collect energy and help to focus it. All good work begins and ends in the here and now.

Day 1- Getting Started

1. Introducing Each Other

Summary

This design is great for newly forming groups. There is always some anxiety and nervousness about meeting a group for the first time and introducing yourself. Often, the anxiety creates a block where many people do not really listen to what their colleagues are saying, and they find they cannot recall much of what was said.

One way to get around this is to have group members introduce one another to the group. Often, introductions are too predictable. This one is a bit different. Asking participants to introduce each other creates a different dynamic of listening and support.

All people love to be interviewed, especially about themselves. This exercise works because it sets up positive pairing subgrouping. There is a feeling of safety and caring that comes through. It becomes evident in the presentation of the other to the group. Watch for the care that gets demonstrated when each pair introduces themselves.

This exercise creates a different form of anxiety (competence) as group members need to "present their partner" to the group. It serves as a nice training experience in taking control of the group and enthusiastically "selling" your partner to the group.

Design and Instructions

Start off by talking about how beginnings are important. Invite everyone to take part by choosing someone they do not know very well, have not worked with, or have not yet met. Have these pairs interview each other with some relevant questions.

Here are some examples:
- What special role will this person fill on the team?
- Ask about some of the talents and skills the person brings to the position.
- What is a special interest or hobby the person pursues after work?
- Is there anything else the person would like the group to know?

Have them interview each other for ten minutes (five minutes a person). Encourage note taking.

After the interview, give them another five minutes to prepare their introductions.

Make sure you emphasize how important it is to introduce their partner with enthusiasm. Allow two minutes per person to introduce.

This exercise is beneficial in so many ways. Using it helps members feel comfortable by giving them a simple task to complete and to appear successful while doing so. It equalizes the risk in the group and creates norms of listening, welcoming, safety, and support. It also gives leaders a chance to welcome others, reinforcing a critical skill.

Time Involved and Ideal Room Set-up
Total Time: For 20 people - 1 hour, 12 minutes
10 minutes to interview each other
5 minutes to prepare their introductions
2 minutes per person to introduce times the number of people
For example, with 20 people it will take 55 minutes
To set this up use the tables in the room to pair up.

Materials Needed for this Exercise
- 2 flip charts for front of room
- Sticky notes

2. Warm-up Exercises

Summary

We believe warm-ups are great when they are done well. Warm-ups must make a point, they should be short, should help encourage interpersonal communication, and they should increase the energy in the room. Warm-ups are also great when used to illustrate a particular idea. Warm-ups can also be useful when you detect a significant lowering of energy. Think about how warm-ups could be used to get the group re-energized and back on task. Here are some other warm-up to become familiar with: Two Truths and a Lie, Clapping and Shaking a Leg, Name your Favorite Things, Dark Side of the Moon, Count to Twenty, etc. Here is a nice opening Warm-up exercise to use:

Behavioral Imagery *(adapted from the Human Element by Will Schutz)*

Design and Instructions
(Use the following introduction imagery if the group is not familiar with this technique or if people are not confident that they will see anything. This sets the stage that there are many ways to imagine, not just visually. If the group is comfortable with imagery you may skip this and go ahead to the "Inclusion" section.)

Find yourself a comfortable place to sit or lie. Shut your eyes and relax. *The following is for purposes of relaxation only.* Scan your body. See if the right side hits the floor the same way as the left side. *10 seconds.* Take a deep breath.

Imagine you are driving down a country road at night. Allow yourself to see the trees and scenery, hear the wind and the motor, smell the air, and feel the steering wheel, seat, and motion of the car. Suddenly, you turn and skid as you round the corner.

Open your eyes. How many people saw a picture of what happened? *Show of hands.* How many people heard the skid? *Show of hands.* How many felt the motion? *Show of hands.* How many smelled the tires? *Show of hands.* We all imagine in different ways. Be attuned to the sensations that you experience as we do the next piece.

Inclusion
Please close your eyes and take a deep breath. Imagine a mountain. See yourself climbing up. As you reach the top of the mountain, you see a group of people coming over the mountain from the other side. Experience this. *20 seconds.*

Notice how it feels to be in that position. Are the people friendly or hostile? Do they come toward you, greet you, avoid you, walk away, or ignore you? *10 seconds.* What do they look like? *10 seconds.* Is there any contact, verbal, or physical? *10 seconds.* How does your body feel? *10 seconds.*

Control
Now imagine yourself becoming much larger than everyone around you. Experience this. *20 seconds.* How does it feel to be much larger? *10 seconds.* Now see yourself becoming much smaller than everyone around you. Experience this. *20 seconds.* How does it feel to be much smaller? *10 seconds.*

Which do you prefer? *10 seconds.* How does your body feel? *10 seconds.*

Openness
Now imagine yourself revealing all your secrets to a group of people. Experience this. *30 seconds.*

Is it frightening or comfortable? *10 seconds.* Are you really telling everything? *10 seconds.* Who are the people in the group? *10 seconds.* How does your body feel? *10 seconds.*

Open your eyes and sit up, please.

Three or four people please tell the group what happened in your imagery. *2 minutes.*

Form trios. Discuss your images and your reactions to them. *5 minutes.* As the facilitator, wander among the trios, picking up the gist of what is being said. Do not be obtrusive but be available. It is useful to do this at all times that the group is divided into small groups. This helps you keep up with what is happening in the group and be more alert to nuances happening in the group.

Now, discuss your main learning from the exercise. *6 minutes.* What does this tell you about your preferences for inclusion, control, and openness?

3. Life Stories

Summary

This design has a rich history. We originally learned it from Elsie Y. Cross, the person who popularized the term "diversity." She made use of it as a way to explore how our early experiences affect our current perception. The exercise is heavy on disclosure, but in the experience, it offers the group the opportunity to open up to feedback, as well. We like to introduce this concept early on as it helps to clarify our goal of creating a safe space where the participants can practice new skills, learn about themselves, take risks, and receive feedback.

This is one of the most powerful exercises in our book. It asks participants to share deeply about themselves with others in the workshop and it creates a safe place for the workshop very early. Some participants are taken back by how deeply they go in sharing their experiences and some suggest this exercise belongs later in the course. Certainly, it would work later in the program. We keep it on the first day because of the norms we want to create. Remember the Maxim, "Groups won't go any further than they will go." You can be assured that the group will self-select how deeply it will allow itself to go. The value to us is that it creates powerful norms of disclosure and feedback.

Over the years, Life Stories has been mentioned over and over as one of the best designs in the laboratory. Please use it with the care that you learned it. It will give you many great memories of your work and it will help others to develop a deeper sense of empathy.

Using the Johari Window Model is a terrific way to introduce this exercise.

Johari Window Design and Instructions

The Johari Window model can also be used to assess and improve a group's relationship with other groups. In 1955 American psychologists Joseph Luft and Harry Ingham devised The Johari Window model while researching group dynamics at the University of California, Los Angeles. It is a valuable tool for understanding:
- Self-awareness
- Personal development
- Improving communications
- Interpersonal relationships
- Group dynamics
- Team development
- Inter-group relationships

It is one of the few tools out there that has an emphasis on behavior, empathy, co-operation, inter-group development and interpersonal development. It is a great model to use because of its simplicity and because it can be applied in a variety of situations and environments.

The Johari Window is useful at the beginning of any gathering that will be focusing on sharing personal information. It offers a clear picture of how relationships grow over time. Some examples:
- Strategic off-sites when introducing new members to teams
- Team building events where the focus will be on deepening discussions between and among team members
- Project debriefs where feedback to team members is emphasized
- Training in the giving and the receiving of feedback

The Lecture Explained
Draw the picture on a flip chart explaining the theory in your own words.

The Johari Window posits that there are four quadrants in any relationship:

The **Open Area** is where I find it is easy and comfortable to share information - ideas and feelings with another. This can be an individual, a team or even an organization.

The **Hidden Area** is where I choose to keep information about myself private. I don't share this with others until I feel it would be useful and until I feel comfortable in doing so. In effect I do my best to hide this information.

The **Blind Area** is where I don't know things about myself but these are apparent to others. Many times it would help me if I became aware of some of the things I do and their affect upon others. Others need to feel comfortable enough with me to tell me these things in a helpful way so that I could understand their effect and have the opportunity to change them should I choose to do so.

The **Unknown Area** is where I don't know why I behave certain ways and neither does the other. We can explore this area with the help of others, professional help, analysis of our dreams, mindfulness etc. The unknown area is not emphasized in our workshop. Pay attention to the feedback you receive from other as this might give you some clues to working in this area.

The dynamic works like this: We can choose to reveal information about ourselves. This is very helpful behavior as it opens ups the hidden area a bit. As we open up the hidden area others tend to reciprocate in either of two ways. They also share from their hidden area and they feel more comfortable giving us feedback about our blind area. In turn we can reciprocate and go deeper.

Learn this explanation and model very well. We find it to be a safe and enjoyable way to start conversations about relationships, building trust, and giving feedback. Learn to draw the simple diagram and fill it in with stories from your own relationship adventures (disclosure).

Johari Window model

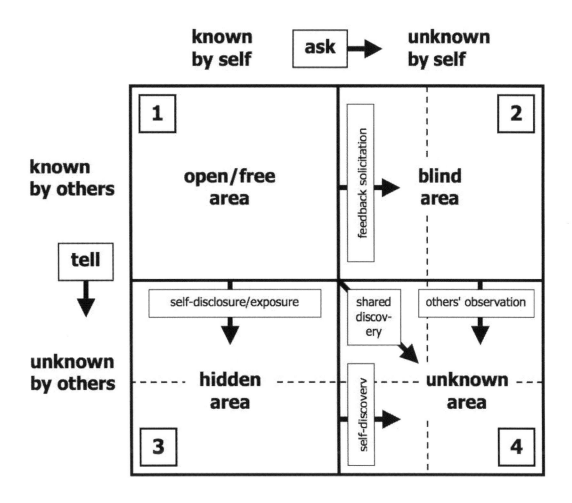

Life Stories Design and Instructions

- After your introduction, hand out index cards.

- Ask the participants to write down seven major events in their lives that have forged them, tempered them, challenged them, and given them pause. Everyone has had major events in their lives that affect them to their core. These could be in the form of teachers, experiences, accidents, achievements, etc. Often these events test one's limits. Coming through the other side of these experiences transforms a person.

- After they write these down, explain they will have seven minutes to talk about their experience to others in the group. The group can only respond by listening deeply and with total attention. After their presentation, the group may give any feedback they wish. You must manage the feedback and the time.

- The exercise should take about a little over an hour. When everyone has understood the directions, give them 10 minutes to write down their seven events. You write yours down as well.

- Divide the group into two groups by counting off.

- The reason we are doing this is because of the time it will take to do the exercise. If this were an intact team, we would not divide the team into two parts.

- Send the groups off and let them manage their own work. Participate fully.

Debriefing the Exercise
Ask open-ended questions about the experience.

Time Involved and Ideal Room Set-up
Total time - 75 minutes based on 16 people
Explain the Johari Window and introduce the exercise - 15 minutes
Group work - Two groups of 8 people 7 minutes each - 60 minutes
Have enough room so that each group can hold their conversations with some privacy.

Materials Needed for this Exercise
- 2 flip charts in the front of the room
- Markers
- Index Cards
- Timer for each group

4. Horse Trading

"Getting the Design that's Best for Me." - Getting your class to volunteer for the exercises and how to set up the feedback process for the facilitators

Summary

Signing up to facilitate the exercises is a critical part of the first day's work in this laboratory. Introduce the exercises by giving a brief introduction to each one and give the homework assignment to look through the "Moving Experiences" book. Having participants choose their preferred design to facilitate increases choice and encourages them to take a risk and try something a bit out of their comfort zone.

In the end this exercise should be fun. It reminds us of a family working on a jigsaw puzzle. Finding the right designs for each participant given the talents and experience within the group is rewarding. It always amazed us how this simple exercise helps to bond the members of the workshop together.

Design and Instructions

- After reading the designs and giving thought to the one or two designs the participants would like to facilitate, this exercise works to get everyone in the class to settle on who will facilitate each design.

- Write down all the names of each of the designs on flip chart paper. We usually put four designs on each page.

- Explain that two facilitators must lead each design. The reason we want two facilitators for each design is to increase collaboration and maximize feedback on performance. It is also more difficult to facilitate with another than to go it alone.

- Hand out two sticky notes per person.

- Each participant places a sticky note with their name on it next to the design they want to facilitate. Let the group do its work and then step back and check to see if each design has two facilitators.

- Trade, and discuss until all the designs are covered.

- Debrief the exercise by discussing how the participants are feeling. Ask if anyone feels uncomfortable with his or her assignment.

- State that this work is not fixed in stone and that up until the next morning they can switch with someone else if the program remains balanced.

This is a fun exercise and it is filled with anticipatory energy. Make yourself available for discussions after the session and for coaching for how to prepare for their assignments.

Time Involved and Ideal Room Set-up
Total time: 20 minutes
We like to post the exercises on a wall and then give our class members a chance to mill about them and discuss possibilities. As you remember from the session, we make use of the sticky notes and encourage everyone to place their notes on the exercises they want to facilitate. This exercise can be continued on the morning of the second day if someone does not own all the designs.

Materials Needed for this Exercise
- 2 flip charts in the front of the room
- Markers
- Sticky flip chart paper
- Post-it Notes

5. Count to Twenty

Summary

At first this design seems silly. Huddling and counting to twenty. As people do it, they really like it. It is simple, but not easy and it does tap into team synergy. This can be a useful warm-up for an afternoon session right after lunch. This is a way to increase awareness in a group and to build relationships. This is a wonderful way for the participants to get in touch with the "Group Mind." The focus of the group on the objective generates a tangible web of connectivity. The group gains a sense of who they are individually and in relation to one another.

Design and Instructions

Count to Twenty calls for a group to stand in a closed circle, with players wrapping their arms around each other's backs – their heads bowed, eyes closed. The players count in turn, with the aim of counting to twenty without anyone saying the same number at the same time. If two or more players voice a number simultaneously, the count begins back at one until the group does the exercise "cleanly."

Coach the players to avoid following a predictable pattern in which the same people claim the same numbers each time (i.e. "I'll always be the one to say two and eight"), but instead to feel the flow between members of the group. Focus on the goal of getting to twenty without two players speaking simultaneously. Try it with a group of four or more players. Newcomers typically stumble through the exercise, while an experienced group who knows one another well can usually Count to Twenty cleanly on the first or second try.

How does the experienced group do it? They do it by connecting, listening, and communicating via what is called in Improv Theater "the Group Mind." The group's focus on the goal generates a tangible (accessible to all the senses) web of connectivity. In "the Group Mind," we gain a sense of who we are – both individually and in relation to one another. In collaborating, rehearsing, and working together, this web of connectedness makes itself present by degrees to the group. The more focused the group is on the objective, the stronger the web – until it becomes more than a way to play the game or perform a scene successfully. It becomes the reason for the game, the scene, and the group to exist. Our feelings about the group and our teammates transform from "otherness" into "oneness."

When players arrive at an understanding of "oneness," they can Count to Twenty on the first or second try with regularity by connecting via this intuitive sense. Finding this state of oneness is vital to an improv group's success in performance. It should come as no surprise that the "feeling of unity" is vital to a successful performance by a business team, as well.

Debriefing the Exercise
- How did you do it?
- Describe your process.
- How could we use this design?
- Did anything get in the way of sensing "the group mind?"

Time Involved and Ideal Room Set-up
Total time: 20 minutes
- The group exercise should take about 10 minutes.
- The debrief could range from 5 to 10 minutes.

You will need some open area to conduct this design as a safe space with enough room to create circles of participants.

Credit for this design goes to Mike Bonnifer of Game Changers

6. Group Dynamics

Summary

This is a classic design that can be modified to fit a number of situations. As you will experience, it is an amazing way to help participants learn how group dynamics affect performance and decision-making. It is compact and powerful and yields the results of a complete semester of group dynamics in a single session. This design pulls together several smaller designs into one involving exercise that emphasizes the paradoxes of group life. They will learn how group dynamics effects performance and decision-making.

We wanted to create an experience that mimics the difficulty of working on project groups where the group meets sequentially, and their present work builds on earlier work. We also wanted to create ambiguous tasks that had to be completed within brief time frames. Finally, we wanted the participants to experience the challenges of group dynamics first hand and observe these challenges from a distance. And so, we settled on the fishbowl design.

Design and Instructions

- Explain that one of the key skills facilitator's need is to be able to read group dynamics and intervene as needed. This design facilitates this learning.
  Note: There is a lot going on here so be sure to keep notes as you go through this exercise.

Setting up the Groups

Learn these instructions well so that they feel natural and you feel comfortable giving them.

- Arrange the chairs in the room so that there are two groups: an inner group and an outer group. The inner group is named "Group 1," while the outer group is "Group 2."
- Divide the group into two groups by counting off in twos. Tell the "1's" to sit in the inner circle and the "2's" to sit in the outer circle.
- Notice you are in two groups. Each group will have two tasks. When you are in the inside group, you will be working on the two tasks simultaneously. When you are in the outside group, you will be observing and critiquing how well the inside group is working.
- This part of the exercise will take 40 minutes. The work will be divided into four rounds for each group. Each group will have 20 minutes to work on the two tasks. An easel pad and markers will be given to you for your work.
- Ask for one volunteer from each group to be "overall process observers." Have these two volunteers sit out of the group on the side. Give each of these observers a **Who to Whom Form** (found in the Appendix).

Problem Solving Stage
The tasks are as follows:
Direct your comments to the inside group.

Inside Group
Task 1
- Please identify the most important skills you believe a person needs to have to be considered competent as a consultant / facilitator.
- Please rank these in importance from most necessary to least necessary.
- Please choose from the list the skills you believe should be emphasized in this workshop.

Task 2
- Do everything in your power to help your team reach high performance during this exercise. Success is defined by how well your team accomplishes both tasks.
- You will work for 5 minutes.

Now direct your instructions to the outside group.

Outside Group
- Your job is to observe and take notes on how well the inside group is performing. Use the Observation form to help you. Hand out the ***Group Observation Form*** and explain that they are to use the form to watch for:
    - Leadership
    - Membership
    - Communication
    - Turning Points

Now direct your instructions to the process observers.

Process Observers
- Instruct the two process observers on the use of the ***Who to Whom Form***. They are to write down the members of their group on the top and the side. They are assigned to watch either Group 1 or Group 2.
- As they observe the group, they are to make a simple tick mark on the form whenever they see that one participant is talking to another.
- At the end of all the rounds they will tally their observations.

Note: When using two facilitators to work this design, one facilitator can give the general directions to the two groups while the other instructs the two process observers how to use the **Who to Whom** forms.

When you are satisfied that both groups understand the task and that the process observers are ready to go, say, "OK, let us begin. Group 1 - on tasks, Group 2 - observe, and process observers start recording."

Timing and Instructions for the Rounds

- Keep strict time. After 5 minutes, stop the groups. Make sure the inside group stops immediately. Ask for 2 minutes of silence.

- Have the groups change seats. The inside group goes to the outside, and the outside group now goes inside. The roles reverse.

- Repeat the instructions from above and keep time.

- After five minutes, go on to Round 2.

- Continue till both sides complete the Four Rounds.

- At the completion of the Four Rounds, have the two groups line up facing each other.

Evaluation of the Group's Performance Stage

- The people who were in Group 1 arrange themselves in a line where they assess as a group how well they performed. Identify one end of the group that stands for low performance and one end of the group that stands for high performance. They form a line indicating how well each person thought the group performed.

- The people who were in Group 2 arrange themselves the way they perceived Group 2 performed.

- Keep it light and laugh about the results.

- Reverse this process, and then discuss the observations and individual learnings.

- Divide the group randomly by counting off into four groups. Each sub group gets one of these topics:
    - Group 1 - Leadership
    - Group 2 - Membership
    - Group 3 - Communication
    - Group 4 - Turning Points

- Have these groups meet for 15 minutes. Share their observations on the topic and prepare a presentation on the highlights: what stood out for them the most in the dimension they discussed.

- Facilitate this discussion.

- End with the process observers sharing their data for Group 1 and Group 2 along with their observations. Process thoroughly.

- Ask about how this design (or parts of it) could be used.

Time Involved and Ideal Room Set-up
Total Time: 1 hour and 30 - 45 minutes
- 10 minutes to explain the exercise and set up the inner and outer circles as well as the two observers flip charts.
- 40 minutes for the inner and outer groups - Four rounds
- 15 minutes for the group to discuss the results of their Group Observations.
- 15 minutes to share the highlights to the group as a whole
- 10 minutes for the process observers to share their results.
  You need a good open area to arrange the chairs in an inner and outer circle.

Materials Needed for this Exercise
- 4 flip charts
- Markers
- Forms – 2 Who to Whom and one for each participant – Group Observation

Day 2 - Action Research

7. Reflections

Summary
Reflections stand for what the participants saw yesterday. The checking-in process is particularly important at the beginning of each day. When done consciously, we welcome everyone to the table (inclusion). We also give everyone a choice about what to share with the group, their readiness for more learning, their perceptions of yesterday, and their expectations for today (control). Finally, it is an invitation to take part fully by contributing and sharing thoughts and feelings as we progress through the exercises (openness). It brings back observations, personal learning, reactions to pieces of the work, and feelings they might wish to share. You are creating norms for safety, participation, and disclosure.

Design and Instructions
When you conduct a "check-in," do it with intent. Bring your full self to the group. Take a moment to compose yourself before starting. Then bring your full energy to the moment. Participants look to the facilitator for cues about energy level, excitement, and interest. What you give, you get.

There are several ways to conduct a check in:
- You can do a "Whip Around," asking your colleagues to share their feelings and their readiness to work today. You can ask if there is anything that could get in the way of their full participation today.
- You can ask the participants to form small groups and then report out to the large group. You are creating norms for safety, participation, and disclosure. The norms formed in the small groups carry over to the large group.

Reflections stand for what the participants saw yesterday in our work together. They are not evaluations. Reflecting brings back observations, personal learnings, reactions to pieces of the work, and feelings they might wish to share. It is done in the moment. Practice helping a group to check-in and make this a part of your routine. It solidifies your role as a facilitator and it can be a great discipline for intact teams to develop, especially on project teams.

Time Involved and Ideal Room Set-up
Total Time 25 minutes for this exercise
15 minutes of discussion from the table groups.
10 minutes for report outs and summary observations.
Set up the room in table groups.

Materials Needed for this Exercise
- Have flip chart and markers ready to capture group reflections.

What is Action Research?

We have placed defining *"Action Research"* on the second day because it allows us to refer back to experiences the participants had on the first day e.g. Life Stories and Group Dynamics. Everything we do with a group is diagnostic. We are always observing, making hypotheses, testing these in real time, and making course corrections.

The Lecture Explained
I draw the *"Action Research"* steps on a Flip Chart and refer to it in my talk. Get your talk down so that you feel comfortable covering this material and taking questions.

Action Research is the foundation of Organization Development.

Here are the steps I name in the talk:
- Entry and Contracting -There is a problem and I can help.
- Define the problem (Jointly).
- Agree to research the problem - interviews, observations, journey maps, surveys, etc. (Jointly).
- Publish the results. This can be done creatively - graphic representation, skits, songs, poems, reports, report outs, fishbowls, or jointly.
- Own the results. Help the group to see their current reality. Everyone owns them.
- Brainstorm Actions - Divergent exercises to Convergent solutions (Jointly).
- Apply the solution, monitor, and continue to research (Jointly).

Make the distinction between Action Research and Scientific Research. In the latter there is a control group and an experimental group. Outside scientists vary conditions on the experimental group and make comparisons. In Action Research we are the experimenters. We are the observers. We conduct research on ourselves. We become the owners of both the experiment and the results.

Note: In our consulting we do not take on the expert role. We help teams, groups, and organizations to design and conduct their own research, so that they do their own work, understand their problems from their perspectives, apply their own solutions, and check their progress. We truly act as facilitators.

Uses
Action Research is fundamental to our work. We make extensive use of it and we teach our clients to have a diagnostic mentality. We teach them to observe group dynamics, raise difficult issues, make conscious decisions, and hold themselves accountable. All the designs in this laboratory are based on Action Research.

Make the Action Research Model part of your thinking and you will be surprised at how often you can make use of it.

8. Singing Our Songs

Summary

In 1980, my team at Shared Medical Systems developed a Leadership program for the company's managers. We wanted a high-energy exercise to kick off the event and send the message that this program was indeed different from any other leadership program our participants may have attended.

The program was residential and began on a Sunday night. We introduced the **Singing Our Songs** exercise as a diagnostic tool and as a way to unite the group through inclusion. The exercise turned out to be quite a hit!

While it provided rich data to work throughout our program, the design also created the means for our managers to define remarkable stories and express them in song with amazing enthusiasm. Unwittingly, we had tapped into a creative force that became part of the lore and history of our Managers' Seminar. At a reunion 25 years later, a small group of folks announced that they wanted to sing their song at the reunion. They brought the house down!

Singing Our Songs links assessment with creativity and joyful participation. This design unites and includes people through song. This is a great diagnostic tool, as it taps into the emotional experience of the participants. It brings honesty to the group through song and humor. This is a powerful exercise. It is a great diagnostic tool, as it taps into the emotional experience of the participants. It has surprising ramifications. Groups are always surprised at the honesty that comes out in song and humor. Make sure you tell the group not to take pictures or videos during the sing along.

This is an Action Research Design as discussed in the introduction for this day. This design allows full participation, so people are included. They have complete control to decide what group issues, history, or concerns they want to illustrate. It is an openness design because they choose the right things to sing about.

Design and Instructions

- Introduce this activity with enthusiasm. Set up the expectations by saying that many cultures use singing as a way to bond workers emotionally as they go about performing difficult tasks. In Japan for example, it is quite common for workers to sing and do calisthenics together before the start of the workday. And in our country, we use singing as an expression of emotion or spirituality (national anthem, hymns, chants, etc.).

- Singing is not typically part of the culture of American corporations, although there are exceptions (Kirby, etc.). In this exercise, we can explore the power of singing together and then discuss how we might use it in helping groups to get what they want.

- When you introduce this exercise, remember that you will be asking people to step a bit out of their norm. So, sell the benefits!

- Have the group count off by threes. This will create three sub groups. Have the new groups sit together. Wait for silence and attention and then proceed.

- Give the groups the following assignment before you assign them a break out room: (You can write these on a flip chart.)
    - "In your small group, define what it was like to work in the culture that embodies your company. What comes to your mind? These should be specific ideas, and you should be able to back up your descriptions with specific examples. Please list at least ten examples."

    - "When you have completed the list, please use the words as lyrics to a song you will create. Attach a melody to your work. **Note:** Most groups choose a melody first. Simple melodies are best. It helps to choose melodies that everyone will likely know."

    - "Write your completed lyrics on newsprint. Your group will lead the larger group in singing your song. Create a song that will not only describe the group's experience of working but will inspire the rest of us as we sing along!"

    - "Explain to the teams that they will have 20 minutes to complete the task. Tell them to have fun and enjoy their work."

- After 20 minutes, reconvene the groups. Have them sit auditorium style in the main room.

- Ask each group to perform its song, and then to lead the entire group through the song.

Debriefing the Session – 10 minutes
This is a high-energy exercise. Groups love to create together and then to perform together. The songs will generate lots of laughter, fun and esprit de corps. Explore a few themes in the discussion.

   Possible Debrief Themes and Questions
   - Creativity - How can you explain the creativity we just experienced after 20 minutes of work?
   - Resistance - Did your group experience any resistance? What form did it

take?

- Practicality - What makes this design always work? What are the dynamics that drive it?
- Relevance - How could we use this design at our organization?

Time Involved and Ideal Room Set-up
  Total Time: 65 minutes
- 5 minutes - Present the design
- 20 minutes - Groups to complete their task
- 7 minutes per group to present. Let us say you have four groups (30 minutes)
- 10 minutes debrief
  Try to create private spaces for the sub groups. If you must do it in one room, have the sub groups retire to the corners. You do not want to ruin the surprise by having the groups know each other's melodies before the presentations.

Materials Needed for this Exercise
- 2 flip charts in the front of the room
- Markers

9. Fairy Tales

Dragons, Elves, Kings, Queens, Witches, Giants, Ogres, and any other creative characters

Summary
This design is a fantastic way to create a useful organizational assessment in the moment. It is subtle and takes a group slightly off balance as it illustrates critical areas for further examination. Over the years this design has proven its worth by surfacing undiscussables in a safe way. The creativity and humor reduce defensiveness that typically interferes with surfacing the issues that needs to be discussed.

The Fairy Tales exercise is especially effective when working with two teams that have conflicts that need to be surfaced and worked. It will always create openings that can be explored in the follow up to the exercise.

This diagram is useful to put on a flip chart for everyone to see. It helps in the crafting of coherent stories that capture the imagination of the group. **Note:** it is also useful to use in debriefing the Group Dynamics Exercise.

Design and Instructions
Introduce the exercise by talking about the structure of a fairy tale. You can begin by announcing to the group that we will be doing an assessment of our organization in a new and creative way.

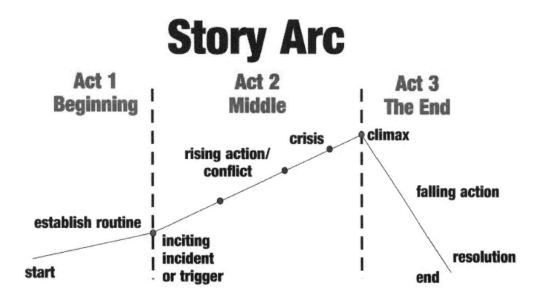

- Ask the group what they know about how a fairy tale is structured. If you only get puzzled looks:

- Ask: "How does a fairy tale begin?"
- Then ask: "And how does a fairy tale usually end?"

- Then suggest that their task is to fill in the middle, but they must write about the themes that are critical for us to examine to improve our work together. Show excitement and enthusiasm for the possibilities of creating our own version of a fairy tale.

- Tell them they can use all the characters usually found in fairy tales. These characters need to be introduced, they need to interact with creative tension, and there needs to be some resolution.

- Give them enough time (usually around 20 minutes) to assess the situation, discuss the possibilities, identify the characters, and draft their story.

- Break them up into small groups - intersperse the leaders so that they are not all in the same group. If you are working with two teams in conflict, mix the groups so that members of each team are in each group. Depending on the size of the group, have at least three subgroups.

- The presentation should be set up as if a parent were reading the tale to their children. A spokesperson reads their work to the group. There will be laughter, high involvement, and deep interest. Do not allow any comments or questions after the story. Go on to the next presentation immediately.

- After they all have been read, ask for general comment. Take a few then move on. Have people count off by threes and get into subgroups. In their subgroups, have them find the underlying themes that need to be discussed and worked by the team to improve their overall productivity, etc.

- Have someone scribe the results. Have a brief discussion of the results.

- Have the group prioritize the themes and then move to a problem-solving activity.

Time Involved and Ideal Room Set-up
  Total time 45 minutes
- 8 minutes - Present the design
- 20 minutes - Groups to complete their task
- 7 minutes per group to present
- 10 minutes debrief

Materials Needed for this Exercise
- 2 flip charts and markers in the front of the room

10. Group Juggling

Summary

This exercise emphasizes how groups learn together to accomplish something that at first seems impossible. It is an especially useful exercise to have in your repertoire, as it is a good beginning for learning how to use any number of experiential exercises. Group Juggling offers a unique way for a group to enter into a playful state while learning. Participants always enjoy this exercise. The answers at the end tend to be highly creative. They illustrate how important it is at times to challenge the rules and to innovate on the spot.

Design and Instructions

Materials Needed

- Three juggle balls - Make sure they are soft, fun to play with, and easy to catch. You also need enough space so that the number of people can stand in a full circle.
- 16 people are about the maximum for this activity. In a large group - say fifty or so, divide the group into four smaller groups, and have them compete against each other.
- You will also need a timer.

- Introduce the exercise by telling everyone we will be learning how to juggle together. We will begin by juggling one ball in a group, and then we will progress to three balls. Tell them that they will be competing against other teams that have gone through this exercise.

- One facilitator stands in the circle, the other is the timekeeper. The one in the circle tells everyone to get ready to learn how to juggle in a group.

- Ask the group members to form a sequence. Say, "I will start the sequence and end the sequence. I will throw the ball to someone in the group. When that person catches it, he or she will throw it to another person in the group who has not caught it before. We will continue until everyone has caught the ball and thrown the ball once. The last person will throw it back to me. When I catch the ball, it will end the sequence."

- After some fumbling and much humor, the group will get the ball to come back home without much trouble. Say, "That was good!" Then, ask your co-facilitator to time the next try and count and errors. Errors are drops or people catching out of sequence.

- The co-facilitator announces the results.

- You say "good job" again. But now you say you will up the ante, by having the group juggle three balls, keeping the sequence the same. All trials will be timed.

- Begin by throwing a ball to the first person in the sequence. Immediately after he or she catches it, throw the second ball, and then the third.

- The co-facilitator announces the time and the number of errors. Usually it is between forty seconds and a minute with at least a drop or two.

- Tell the group "good job" and then turn to the co-facilitator and ask what the best-known time for this exercise is. The co-facilitator answers that the <u>world record is less than 3 seconds with no drops.</u>

- Tell the group you will give them 4 minutes to make a dramatic change in their time. The only rules are that the sequence must not change, and they must touch all the balls. Give them the four minutes and do not help them. Observe what they do.

Presentation of the Solution
Have the group present their solution and have the co-facilitator time it. If they have broken the world record - less than three seconds with no drops - celebrate! If not have them try again and encourage them to change their solution.

Note on the Solution
Over the years, we have seen many different solutions. They all are incredibly creative. There are a few that get it done in less than three seconds. About 85% of the time the group will figure it out. Let them have a go at it. At the end we can show some of the great solutions.

Debriefing the Exercise
Debriefing this exercise takes some focus and some thought. If it is not done well, the exercise will just come off looking like a game. Here are some questions you could ask the group:
- What did you learn from this experience?
- What made it easy to experiment?
- How did humor and play influence the outcome?
- How can we apply our learning to real work experiences?
- How did leadership occur?

Time Involved and Ideal Room Set-up
Total time: 25 minutes
5 minutes to introduce the exercise.
10 minutes for the group juggle.

5 -10 minutes to debrief.

Have enough room for your group to be able to freely move about have their circle.

Materials Needed for this Exercise
- 3 juggle balls /16 people
- Timer

11. Real-Time Interviews

Summary

I learned this technique over 30 years ago. I have used it extensively for helping groups create strategy, assess their current reality, and create meaningful conversations that translate into action. The design is known for its consensus-seeking outcomes. It is remarkably high on inclusion and openness. Over the years, the Real-Time Interviews (RTI) technique has evolved. We have learned to be very flexible in how to set up this experience and how to facilitate it. In the workshop, we will cover many ways to apply it. This technique scales really well. We have conducted this exercise for up to 500 people. You need trained facilitators for each room of 50 participants.

At the end of this session you will have learned how to design, structure, and facilitate a Real-Time Interview Session.

This is a classic Action Research design, and one you should incorporate into your facilitation practice. RTI is simple yet complicated in the mechanics. It is one of the most beautiful designs I have ever seen. Learning it well will pay you back one hundred-fold. The power of this design comes from the questions that are developed by the group. It is essentially a real-time assessment of the group's current reality. After publishing the data, the group will transform the data into "live" information. Their new understanding will create a group need to resolve the issues raised. Your job as a facilitator is to keep the process moving and to allow the discovery that occurs to unfold, naturally. This design always generates enormous positive energy.

The design Real-Time Interviews is pure Action Research. The group develops the questions. The group answers the questions. After they publish the answers you let them figure out what it all means. They will love doing it, and in the process, they will seek a consensus and evaluate their own results.

Design and Instructions
Plan in Advance - Developing the Questions

The critical questions are developed beforehand. Usually this occurs in the contracting session. You can sit down with the team leader and/or company owner and brainstorm several questions that they feel need to be asked to the group.

Creating the final questions is as much art as it is science. Questions need to be focused, yet open-ended. They need to be relevant, and they should invite the participants to think deeply about the issues. Here are some sample questions that we have found to be helpful in the formulation of your questions:

- Please identify several accomplishments you are most proud of as a member of this team. Please be specific.
- Given our position in the market and our most recent offer, what keeps you up at night? What might we not be seeing?
- If you were the leader of this team, please name three things you would focus on to help us become even more productive.
- From your perspective, what are some ideas that must be included in our new vision? Please be specific.
- Name three to five ideas or suggestions that you believe would help us to become more agile and flexible in our response to our customers.
- What are some of the most key factors that are causing the resistance to our proposed changes?

Your job first and foremost is to decide how many questions will be asked and how many small groups you will have. We like to have no more than five questions in our sessions. The reason is that you must think about presenting the data back. The general rule is: five presentations are about the maximum a group can process at one time. If you go over five, you risk watering down the report outs by overwhelming the group with the data. We have included specific instructions to the facilitators on how to run this exercise in this handbook.

Secure the Buy-in of the Leadership

Make sure the team leader or leadership team is involved throughout the Real-Time Interview process to insure they will support the results and data that come out of this exercise. They should be part of the team that formulates the questions to be asked, be a participant in the interview process, and sit in to hear and offer perspectives on the ultimate results of the theme team. You want to create key places for their insight and input as well as build-in their support when it is time to hear the results and to implement the suggestions and ideas.

Often before an RTI session we call the group together, inform them about the process, and ask those attending to help us develop mission-critical questions that the entire group should answer. A great question to ask the assembled team is "what are the questions we should be asking ourselves?"

For our purpose, we will be demonstrating the technique using four questions. We will determine the four questions for this exercise together.

Part 1: Setting up the Room in Advance

> **The Pre-prepared Flip Charts:**
> - Each question is written out on separate flip chart page and hung on the wall.

- The time sequence and the major activities are written on a flip chart and posted.

- Definition of Truths, Trends, and Unique Ideas is written out and hung on the wall:
    - **Truths** are defined as a statement that everyone you interviewed made. For example, on a given question you interviewed three people and three out of three said the same thing. This is a "truth."
    - **Trends** were not as consistently stated as truths. Only two out of three said it. You declare it a "trend."
    - **Unique Ideas** are just that - one person said it, and you feel it is important for the group to hear, so you declare it a "unique idea."

- A separate flip chart (4) and a set of markers for each of the question group discussions. Write the number and each question on the front top of the page. Place the five flip charts into position in advance.

The Pre-prepared Questions for the Chairs
- Have the prepared questions written out in advance on either an index card along with 4 blank cards per participant or preprinted inside a small stenographer's notebook.

Set the room up according to the following diagram:

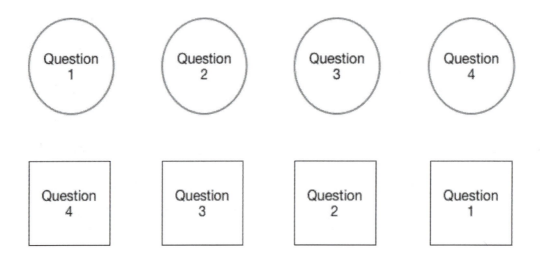

Arrange the chairs in the room as pictured. Place either the pre-prepared stenographer's notebook with the questions or the index cards with the questions and three-five more index cards and a pencil on each chair face down on the chairs as shown in Diagram above.

Part 2. Explaining the Design to the Participants, and Conducting the Interviews

Invite the participants into the room and direct them to fill in the chairs - there can be no gaps. Tell them to pick up the card/notebook on the chair, the pencil, and the extra cards. Do not start until all chairs are filled.

Give your version of the following statement: "We are going to learn a technique called Real-Time Interviews. Please follow along and experience the entire technique. Afterwards, we will discuss its application."

Explain that everyone has a card/notebook with a question on it. In this exercise, each participant will ask this question to four other people. They are to take notes using the other cards/notebook. There will be four rounds. In each round, the Circles will ask the Squares their question first. The Squares will have two minutes to answer the questions.

When two minutes have elapsed, the Squares will ask their question to the Circles. At the end of two minutes the first round is over.

Think Speed Dating. At the end of the round, ask the Squares to move one seat to their right. The Square with Question #4 in the top half of Diagram 1 will move to the seat across from the Circle with Question #2, and so forth. The Square with Question #1 would now sit across from the Circle with Question #1. The interview process would begin again as in round 1 - two minutes for the Squares, and two minutes for the Circles. The concept of "musical chairs" will help the group understand what to do.

Note: During the exercise, each person will also answer the question he or she is asking.

Repeat the process until the final fourth round. Keep strict time. Helpful hint: Draw the diagram on a flip chart and show the people how to move. Remember - the Circles never move!

Part 3: Having the Individuals Organizing their Data

Following the interviews, ask each person to sit in silence for 5 minutes and make sense out of their data. One way to do this is to use the technique **Truths, Trends, and Unique Ideas.** This technique is especially helpful when the group is larger and when you are asking more questions. So, learn it now!

Truths are defined as statements that everyone you interviewed made. For example, on a given question you interviewed three people and three out of three said the same thing. This is a "truth."

Trends were not as consistently stated as truths. Only two out of three said it. You declare it a "trend."

Unique Ideas are just that - one person said it, and you feel it is important for the group to hear, so you declare it a "unique idea."

The questions you will be asked most frequently are: What is a truth? What is a trend? And, "How do you tell the difference between a Truth and a Trend?" We always restate the instructions, Truths are those answers that everyone has said and you yourself agree with as well. Trends are not as strong as truths. Help them to be flexible about their definitions. Have the definitions written out on a flip chart in front of the room.

Sometimes there can be a common theme across questions. If this occurs three times it is a "Super Truth". "Super Truths" are critical issues to pay attention to and address.

Take five minutes to do this task in silence.

Part 4: Consensus and Presentations
Ask all the people who had the same question form separate groups. Thus, everyone with Question #1, assemble here, Question #2 here, etc.

Give them the following instructions:
- Assign each group a room. Have them appoint a scribe and in the case of a large-scale Real-Time Interview, have a data manager for each group to capture the results on a computer to ease the consolidation of the responses for the Theme team.

- Tell them to meet and reach a consensus on what everyone said in response to their question. They should use Truths, Trends, and Unique Ideas. Write the results on a flip chart.

- When they have finished the written part of this assignment, they must construct a creative way to introduce their report to the group. It can take the form of a skit, a song, a poem, etc. It must be a thematic summary of their data. Tell them they have 20 minutes to complete both parts of this assignment. **Note:** In a real meeting with larger numbers, this time frame would be longer.

At the end of the time, bring the groups back together and have them sit auditorium style. Call for presentations. Skit or song goes on first. Next, they present the data. Finally, they open a discussion. Facilitate the discussion.

For a large group (50-500 people) you can form a "theme team" (one person volunteers from each room). This group will work the results from similar multiple groups to consolidate the data and present back to the entire group the following day. In the large meeting of the whole, the most compelling themes are called "Super Truths." In this instance it is recommended that the leadership team is present at the end of the Theme Team consolidation process to hear the results. This will give them time to prepare a response to the whole group for the next day.

Part 5: Additional Tips
- There are variations to setting up this exercise. Once, I was surprised to learn that our room was changed just before I arrived. I found myself in a room filled with exceptionally large and difficult to move easy chairs. There were 24 people, four topical areas, and there were still three questions for each interviewer to ask. I simply paired everyone up with three different people. They interviewed each of the persons according to a schedule I drew out on a flip chart. I kept time. After each four minutes, I directed them to either reverse the interview process (allow themselves to be interviewed or move on to their next person). This took some last-minute legwork to set up the diagram, but it worked perfectly.

- Make sure you greet and usher everyone in the seats before you begin.

- Break out rooms for the groups are not necessary, but the subgroups should be separated in the large room when reaching consensus on their question.

- Participants can take a coffee break when doing their individual work. Make sure you check this time so that you do not go over the allotted time you set.

A Word about Skits
When we facilitate "Real-Time Interviews" we have asked the sub groups to present a critical piece of the data they collected in the form of a skit. Skits cut to the core. They create a vivid picture of the data, and it is usually humorous. After six weeks have gone by, people barely remember the meeting they attended. What they do remember is the skit that was presented. And the memory will ignite some questions about what happened and how are they are progressing.

Skits also involve everyone in the subgroup. They call for the leaders to play publicly. The humor is contagious and helps create a safe and relaxed atmosphere conducive to action planning. Allow the participants to find or create props. All of this adds to the excitement and enjoyment at the end of the exercise.

Debriefing the Exercise
- First, ask what everyone thought of the exercise. Lead an open discussion.
- Make sure everyone understands the mechanics.

- Ask how they might use it.
- Ask why it works.

- What are the structural dynamics that make this a consistent winner?
- Open a discussion about how the design follows the principles of Action Research.

Time Involved and Ideal Room Set-up
Total time 2 hours
- 15 minutes - Organize and seat the participants
- 5 minutes - Introduce the exercise and give instructions
- 25 minutes - The Real Time Interviews (each timed sequence is 5 minutes for a total of 25 minutes)
- 10 minutes - Alone Time to Organize the Data
- 30 minutes - Group Discussions by Question
- 30 minutes - Presentation of Truths, Trends and Unique Ideas to the Group (30 minutes - each group has 6 minutes each)

You need a good-sized room for each of the interview groups.
All the set up should happen before the exercise begins.

Materials Needed for this Exercise
- 6 flip charts in the (2) front of the room (4) break out groups
- Markers
- Sticky flip chart paper
- Pencils/pens
- Index cards/steno pads

See the Appendix for Instructions to Facilitators and a set of drawings on how to set up the rooms.

12. Rotational Action Planning

Summary

This design saves time at strategic off-sites and it makes effective use of the fundamental human motivations of inclusion, control, and openness. It is useful for the ending of a team building session or a strategic planning meeting. Anytime a group creates action plans and wants an inclusive review of them, think about applying this design. It is simple and robust and allows for an elevated level of interaction. Groups work in their first group and then edit the work of the other groups. It is important to note in their editing that they can add and suggest but not eliminate the ideas of the others.

We often employ this design after we get our results from the Real-Time Interview exercise. Have the group prioritize the results from the session. You can do this by any means you choose. Show off your skills by creating a way to prioritize the results quickly into three action-planning teams. Assign people to these teams. Again, use your own ideas about how to create these groups.

This design is also useful at process improvement sessions, and brainstorming meetings. We also use it for creating customer Journey Maps where small groups work on the separate experiences the customer has as they take part in your offer e.g. Marketing, Sales, Purchase, Use, Return Customer.

Design and Instructions

The facilitators decide upon a topic, issue, or concern they want the group to deal with, such as the results from the Real-Time Interviews. Have the class divide into three groups by counting off. The assignment is to have these groups discuss, develop, and agree upon an action plan.

- Once in the sub-groups, have the group appoint a scribe/historian. Their job will entail using a flip chart to capture the thoughts on the actions that might be taken to move forward.
  Typically, action planning includes:
  - The actions
  - The person(s) accountable for carrying out the action
  - A completion date

- Have each of the groups list their ideas and actions. After 15 minutes, ask the scribe-historian to stay in their group and have each team rotate to another group.

- Once everyone has rotated, begin the process again. The scribe-historian recounts the ideas, the actions, the leader, and the completion date. Reduce the time by ten minutes for this round. The new group can edit by adding ideas and actions but cannot take away any actions.

- Rotate through the final time. Set the time for 10 minutes, the same as the last round.

- Assemble the groups in their original teams and allow them time to polish their final presentation. Allow ten minutes.

- Present results and call on the scribes-historians to comment on the groups that they did not get to participate in during rotations. Allow 5 minutes for each group to present.

Time Involved and Ideal Room Set-up
Total Time is group size dependent
As with so many experiences, timing is everything. Be sure to keep the groups to their time limits. We make the first group session longer than those that come after.
- 7 minutes to explain the exercise.
- 15 minutes for original group, then 10 minutes each for each rotational group. If there were three rotating groups that would take 35 minutes. You can go up to six groups.
- 10 minutes for the original group to polish their final presentation.
- Whatever time each group needs to make the final presentation, usually 5 minutes each.
- If you have a larger group, with multiple rooms and multiple questions then you need a data manager with a computer to capture the information along with a scribe and an historian.

Materials Needed for this Exercise
- Flip charts for each group
- Markers

Day 3 – Innovation Theme

13. The Impact Wheel

Summary Innovation Theme
The third day of the Laboratory is focused on designs that help teams to think creatively and to explore techniques for making better decisions. The mental models that we all use to hold structure or own approaches to problem solving and decision-making. Challenging our mental models is often difficult because we have to shift our perspective and try to see things differently. An example of this is to look at a tree. We know it is a tree because of the patterns we see. A way to see a tree differently is not to look "at the tree," but to look at the spaces in-between the branches. Try to see these spaces as a whole and not the tree. It is hard to hold this new perspective.

Summary the Impact Wheel
The Impact Wheel introduces us to some new ways of thinking. The exercise looks easy at first. As you try to imagine impacts the thinking becomes more difficult. It is possible to discover new ways of thinking about decisions that are being considered. It is also a wonderful way to analyze events that are trending in the marketplace, with competitors, customers, suppliers etc. The Impact Wheel is most helpful in discovering unintended consequences about actions you are considering.

The theory behind this design is one that challenges our mental models. We often have a default scenario in our heads about a particular situation and how we think it will unfold. Cognitive dissonance theory holds that we tend to see things we already believe will happen (believing is seeing). The Impact Wheel allows a group to see and then say impacts that might be unlikely but highly consequential should they ever happen.

The Impact Wheel is an excellent multi-purpose forecasting tool. It can be applied in many situations when it is necessary to search for or discover impacts and implications that are non-obvious. The purpose of the Impact Analysis Wheel is to explore the realm of the possible and to increase the participants' awareness of potential implications. Moreover, it is a multiple "right answer" tool. Use it to explore the possible implications of a trend, innovation, goal, policy, or any decision that is about to be made.

I learned this design from a Japanese consultant who was working for Kodak. At the time, we were helping the organization assess the possible impact of the up-and-coming digital revolution. We have all seen the results of that, and Kodak was asking the right questions at that time.

It involves picking a "trigger statement" and looking at the impacts of that statement for a business. It is useful for many things: environmental scanning, unintended consequences, etc. I was at a session recently when the group decided to look at the impact for 10,000 people retiring in the US every day for the next 18 years.

Specifically, the Impact Analysis Wheel is a small group technique (four to ten people), which can be used successfully to ease participants out of thinking about a problem, goal, or situation in a linear fashion. Rather, the group is required to approach the problem statement holistically, and then work towards alternatives in a concentric fashion. Be careful, the trigger question needs to be able to focus the group on the impacts that could happen.

Design and Instructions

For constructing the Impact Wheel, the steps are outlined below:

- Divide the group into fours by counting off. Give each group a flip chart and a marker and a pack of sticky notes for each person. Have the groups work for 20 minutes and then return. Each group must choose a spokesperson to explain their Impact Wheel, tell their story, and identify what they are learning about the possible impacts.

- Have each group choose one of the following sample trends to explore or make up your own to fit the group:
  - 10,000 people retire everyday
  - Advanced robotics are changing the manufacturing and service sectors
  - The drought and water shortage are extended in the western U.S.
  - Solar panels are now fully transparent

- A statement is placed in a circle (hub) in the middle of a large white wall (this could also be a large sheet of paper). The assumption is made that the trend (or whatever is in the circle) will continue.

- Each participant is given a pack of sticky notes. The participants are asked to name immediate, direct consequences of the "trigger statement" that has been placed in the circle (hub). These are the first order impacts. The only restrictions are that the ideas generated are possible and direct (first order) in nature.

- Next, a second order circle (hub) is drawn around the first order impact and then ideas are generated for each first order impacts identified in the circle. Each first order impact is considered individually, but not necessarily, in order of original creation. Develop at least two new impacts, looking for both positive and negative possibilities. These are the "impacts of impacts."

- If there is time, continue this process through the third and fourth orders of impact. Same or similar impacts may appear more than once, on the same level or various levels. It is OK to be humorous and even off-the-wall. Remember that this is an exploratory analysis.

- Tie the impacts together whenever a natural, dynamic feed situation seems to occur. This is done with a single line from one impact to another. You may cross-levels and you may give the line a directional flow indication if appropriate. The idea is to develop stories and or possible scenarios.

- A single application of this technique will not uncover a complete set of possible impacts. It is particularly useful to have more than one group examine the same statement and then compare the results. No two wheels will be exactly alike, even though there may be some overlap. Multiple wheels produced on the same topic increase the chances of discovering a larger range of possible impacts.

Debriefing the Exercise
- How can this design be used in your organization? Where and with whom?
- Did you experience any difficulties with the exercise? Why? What happened?
- Ask your own questions.
- **Note:** it is helpful to use Hexagon sticky notes for this exercise.

Time Involved and Ideal Room Set-up
Total Time: 1 hours plus more
We like to give at least an hour to this exercise if we are doing it at a strategic offsite. Senior teams often will take more time, especially if they discover something critical. When you are teaching this technique it often takes a bit longer because of settling on trigger questions. Have a few trigger questions ready to use as examples.

A large room is ideal for this work. We often make use of one room and put the small groups in the corners, so they will not be distracted by the other groups.

Materials Needed for this Exercise
- Flip charts for each group or large paper
- Markers
- Sticky Notes

14. Digital Decision-Making

Summary

We make use of Digital Decision-Making frequently, especially at strategic off-sites. It is a useful way to identify the core elements that the group is using to make a decision and to see what weight the group is giving to each of these elements. Digital Decision-Making is a good discipline for leaders to have in their back pocket to help them determine how their group is viewing upcoming decisions. It is also useful to help groups to follow their own logic and challenge their own thinking about what they believe will happen once the decision is made.

Digital Decision-Making is designed to find the core elements for any important or mission critical decision. Many times, groups make decisions without applying a consistent logical process. This encourages "group think" and leads to less ownership of the ultimate decision by the group members i.e. "Mistakes were made, but not by me." A well-facilitated Digital Decision-Making session reduces the chances of low-quality decision-making. It also will show if there any core elements that need further research. Often, discovering areas for additional research adds excellent value to the group's decision-making process.

We learned this technique from Robert Fritz, and it is a great one. It is enormously powerful designs for helping teams make critical decisions. The key is to introduce the concept, work with an example, and then let the team members try it for themselves. Digital Decision-Making is a rigorous and structured way to facilitate a group's decision-making. Usually it takes about twenty minutes to a half-an-hour to learn the technique. It has many applications.

Design and Instructions
Background Explanation for the Facilitators
Trigger Decision

To set up this design, there needs to be a **Trigger Decision** and you need to frame it as a two-way, digital outcome. A trigger decision is defined as the starting point for digital decision-making. It is the focus of what the group is trying to decide. It is stated as an alternative of two possibilities.
Examples:
1. Buy or build
2. Invest additional funds - Yes or No
3. Get married or put the wedding off
4. Buy a new car or buy a used car

In analog decision-making we can go around and round about these decisions and create noise as we attempt to decide. Often this leads to confusion and getting lost in the weeds. Analog decision-making can be a way of avoiding conflict and delaying important decisions. Digital Decision-Making changes all this.

Rules of Two's and Three's
Rule of Two's (2's) and Three's (3's) - We first have the group define their **Core Elements** that underscore or make up the decision. We reduce each of the core items to either two choices / outcomes or three choices / outcomes.

The first rule is to have the final decision be a decision of only two possible courses of action - Yes or No, for example. We represent this decision as the following:

(+ -)

Core Elements
Next, we identify the Core Elements that make up the decision. These are the elements that we must consider in making our decision.

For example, if we were trying to decide whether to buy a car or not, we might consider:
- Budget / Price - Does the price fit our budget? This would be a two (Yes or No).
- Practical use - Practical Value. This would be a three (high, medium, low).
- Timing- When do we need this car? This would be a two (now, when).

Facilitate a discussion right now on the Amy and Ted example below. It is a lot of fun and illustrates Digital Decision-Making in a unique way. Break the group up into small groups and have them practice Digital Decision-Making with this example using the method described above.

The Story of Amy and Ted
A while ago, we hired an apprentice to work with us and learn facilitation. She was enormously talented and learned very quickly. About 6 months into her term, I found her upset and a bit out of sorts. Concerned, I asked her what was wrong. She said she was having a challenging time making her mind up about marrying Ted, her boyfriend. Amy and Ted had been dating for over a year. Ted was committed, while Amy was not so sure. Amy had been married once before, and according to her, the experience was a disaster. At the time, she had a 10-year-old son, and he and Ted got along great. Ted was getting his PhD in Math, though it was taking him much longer than expected. Ted and Amy were not living together.

Use Digital Decision-Making to analyze the scenario. Note that this decision took 20 minutes when we did it with Amy. So, did she marry Ted?

- What are the **Core Elements** that Amy might consider about her relationship with Ted? Ask the group for input. Please scribe the elements on a flip chart. Make sure you get about 6-8 elements.

- Now **apply the rule of Two's and Three's**.
  Each element can have either two alternatives or three alternatives. That is the rule. Have the group agree on whether each element is a two alternative decision or a three-alternative decision.

Pick someone to be Amy. Turn the flip chart around. Have Amy circle the elements according to how she feels now. Then turn the flip chart around.

Amy's Dilemma
    Did Amy and Ted get married? (Y - N)

Bring the entire group back to discuss their charts and the decisions they explored. How could this technique be used? Ask about practical applications.

Time Involved and Ideal Room Set-up
Total Time: One hour
Prep the facilitators ahead to keep their introductory remarks short - 10 minutes so that the group can experience playing with developing the core elements and applying the rule of two's or three's.

Materials Needed for this Exercise
- 1 Flip chart in the front of the room and flip charts for each group
- Markers

15. The Virtual Hive

Summary

We branded "The Virtual Hive" from GroupMind software, a subsidiary of Monarch Media. In this workshop we will give a short demo of The Virtual Hive to show you what is possible and where the field is going. We firmly believe that Kurt Lewin would have been all over this software!

OD practitioners designed GroupMind with experienced facilitators to accelerate feedback cycles and deepen group discussions. Using it allows us to collaborate both face-to-face and remotely by using some remarkably simple tools. The Virtual Hive is a simple set of powerful web tools that work silently in the background of your meeting. Your meeting content remains first and foremost. The Virtual Hive allows you to add an interactive dimension to your meetings easily and quickly.

The Virtual Hive saves money, reduces time, and increases productivity exponentially at meetings. For example, before going to break outs, the participants can brainstorm ideas for each break out instantly. When the groups break out they will have a great start based on the ideas of all the participants. And because we network the entire meeting, there is no need for those paper flip charts. We eliminate all the paper and make your meeting less paper dependent. Everything is saved and retrievable after the meeting. We eliminate all the typing of flip charts and the time wasted putting them into a readable format.

Action Research is behind GroupMind Software. It was designed to brainstorm and then show the results instantly and if you want, anonymously. Groups can use it to do research on themselves in the form of brainstorms, surveys, discussions, voting, ranking, etc. GroupMind incorporates all the requirements for Action Research. It levels the playing field by having everyone take part instantly. Publishing is easy - just click "Group Mind" and the thoughts of everyone can be seen. These results can then be jointly ranked and sorted, owned, and understood. From there the group can create action plans and monitor their results.

With The Virtual Hive you can collect comments and feedback instantly from any group, at any time and any place. You can:
- Brainstorm
- Vote
- Prioritize
- Hold discussions
- Survey

Design and Instructions

Your audience can use their smart phones, e-readers, tablets, and laptops. All they need is a device that can connect to the Internet. Bring Your Own Device (BYOD) is how we describe these meetings to participants. Each Hive meeting is designed with the help of our meeting consultant. Together with you we design a series of interactive exercises that fit seamlessly into your presentation.

The Virtual Hive is made for meeting participation. By using it you can transform your static, one-way communication meeting into:
- An interactive event that engages and excites your audience
- Turn your passive audience into active participating members and give a voice to introverts and extroverts alike
- Level the playing field by enabling every opinion to count

The Hive is great for engaging, aligning, and unifying your team, department, or organization.

GroupMind can be used in about any design that you would do face-to-face. It can be used for:
1. Innovation circles - moving from brainstorming (divergent thinking) to prioritizing (convergent thinking).
2. Pre-meeting surveys
3. Displaying data collected (flip charts)
4. Prioritizing work
5. Weighted voting (similar to using Avery dots.
6. Hosting discussions
7. Storing articles and documents
8. Displaying slide shows (can be followed by open commenting)
9. Creating action planning
10. Using a matrix to display data (spreadsheets)
11. Confidence checks at strategic off-sites
12. Change management - surfacing resistance

Time Involved and Ideal Room Set-up

In using GroupMind, most of the time is used in building an agenda for your work. Your actual time teaching will be determined by how complex your demo will be.

In our work, we usually take about 45 minutes to do a demonstration. This includes: brainstorming, discussion, survey, ranking, and voting.

If you want to learn more about The Virtual Hive, please contact us at: rob@robertmcneil.com

16. Concordant Decision-Making

Summary

Concordant Decision-Making was designed to improve the follow through on critical decisions. We like to use it to move beyond consensus so that it is clear what decision was made, the entire group agreed with the decision, and the entire process was open and transparent. We teach it to Senior Teams who want a way to align their members to a decision and have them commit to its implementation. Concordant Decision-Making is not to be taken lightly.

Concordant Decision-Making is adapted directly from Will Schutz's FIRO - Human Element Theory. This is a powerful technique that can be extremely useful to help groups make critical decisions. Learn this technique and keep it in your pocket. You never know when you might need it.

Design and Instructions

We can learn this technique by looking at decision-making. Groups usually have their way of making decisions wrapped in their norms, and these are typically unstated or unchallenged.

There are a few classic decision-making processes:
- The leader makes the decision unilaterally
- The leader listens to the team and then makes the decision
- The team discusses the decision and then votes.

A facilitator or leader works with the group to achieve consensus and they decide together. All of these methods work and are useful. They all have variations and they can weigh different criteria in diverse ways. Will Schutz recommended a method for critical decisions that goes beyond consensus and he named it Concordance Decision-Making.

Concordance has these three essential components:
- Everyone affected by the decision must be involved in making the decision (Inclusion)
- Anyone can veto the decision (Control)
- Everyone must be willing to state their reasoning and their feelings to the group about the decision (Openness)

Note: If people cannot attend the decision meeting they give up their veto power and acknowledge that the group can make this decision without them - no proxies allowed.

We poll the group by setting up the decision to be made in simple and direct language. We phrase the question in the affirmative. We ask everyone to affirm the statement publicly: "I support moving ahead on (insert statement)."
- We explore any and all differences and the veto's
- Everyone must be in the affirmative before we move forward
- If we cannot move forward, we list what must be worked, and further researched. We table the decision until we reconvene

In our session, we will create a faux decision and you and your partner will facilitate an open discussion using Will's principles. Enjoy!

Time Involved and Ideal Room Set-up
Total time: One hour
You will need enough time to practice making a concordant decision. You can role-play a decision.

17. The Executive Here and Now

Summary

This is an advanced intervention you can employ to help teams learn to work in the present. It is one of the best trust-building activities for intact teams. We make use of it when teams invite us to become coaches to them on the way to high performance.

When you look at the Drexler Sibbet Model you will see that there is an arrow that shows that high performance is directly related to trust. This is not to be taken lightly. As teams approach high performance, intimacy goes way up. Team members become close and they become aware of the feelings and needs of the others on the team. They can even anticipate what needs to be done. Synergy and intimacy are closely related.

Design and Instructions

By asking team members to give this a try, you can create the possibility of team members entering into a deeper conversation. Ask the group if they would like to give this a try.

Then ask for eight volunteers. Employ the fish bowl technique to run this exercise. Ask for the eight volunteers to join you in the inner circle. Ask for the participants on the outside to observe the conversation and to take some notes about what they see.

On the inside, write on a flip chart the following:
Encounter
- Be open and honest
- Talk about your feelings
- You are responsible for yourself
- Be in the Here and Now
- Try to say what needs to be said
- If you do not like what is happening, do something about it

Run the session for twenty minutes. Keep time.
Debrief the experience (fifteen minutes total), switching the groups.

Time Involved and Ideal Room Set-up
Total time: 45 minutes

Materials Needed for this Exercise
- 2 flip charts in the front of the room
- Markers

18. Cover Story

Summary

This design is one of our favorites. It always energizes the group by exploring what is possible. Once these ideas are presented the team can work backwards to see how it got there. It is a particularly effective way to reduce defensiveness about future endeavors while increasing innovative thinking with fun collaboration. Cover Story is a wonderful way to begin action planning at a Strategic off-site.

This is a brilliant design to have in your back pocket. We have used it countless times, often at strategic off-sites. Leaders need a way to escape their own perceptions of their current reality and to dream about possibilities. This is one way to do that. You can vary the instructions by creating a wall chart or having people draft stories about their future. Groups love doing this exercise. Creating the ideal future is exciting, fun, and involving.

We use Cover Story from The Grove Consultants: https://grovetools-inc.com/collections/cover-story-vision

Design and Instructions
- Divide the large group into four teams
- Make sure the leaders are split up among the subgroups
- Give each group a large piece of graphic paper

Give some sort of variation of the following instructions:
It is three (this number can vary) years from now. Your organization has been written about by the Wall Street Journal (or any other trade journal connected to their field). You have accomplished what no one believed possible, and the article is describing what happened and how these amazing goals were achieved. There are several headings to have the group consider.

The Headline - Pithy and catchy, the headline summarizes the great accomplishment.
By-lines - The story of how the team succeeded. These create interest and motivation in terms of what is possible.
Quotes – These quotes should bring in the voices of the leaders and are a true call to action. Surprisingly, they also subtly offer encouragement to the current leaders. There is a natural, creative sense of humor that is unleashed by these quotes.

With a large piece of paper, you can have people in small groups sketch out the story. At the end, you can have a walk around and have each subgroup present its Cover Story.

Time Involved and Ideal Room Set-up
   Total time one hour
The introduction should be about seven to ten minutes, the work in small groups takes about 20 minutes, and the presentation takes another 15 - 20 minutes. Debrief for a final 10 minutes.

Materials Needed for this Exercise
- 1 Cover Story per sub group
- Markers

Day 4 - Teams and the Matrix

19. Drexler Sibbet Team Assessment

Summary

The Drexler Sibbet Team Performance Model is central to this laboratory workshop. Besides being a model and a map, it is also a great backdrop for all the facilitation designs. The model is based on a working theory of groups and group dynamics developed over 30 years ago by Alan Drexler and David Sibbet. It serves as a lexicon for talking about teams, team development, and team start-ups. It can also be used as a highly effective team assessment as described in this design. In our consulting practice we make extensive use of the Drexler Sibbet Model with our clients.

Using the Drexler Sibbet Model for a team assessment creates the possibility for a robust discussion of the team's history, its current reality, and the actions team members could take to help them improve their team's performance. The assessment can be as simple as the one we use in this design, or it can be formalized by using the Drexler Sibbet Team Performance On-line Team Assessment. Using the formal assessment requires getting certified as a team consultant. If you are interested in becoming certified, please contact us for this information.

Group dynamics theory lies behind this model. It derives from the study of groups and organizations that followed from the original work of Kurt Lewin and his followers as they developed and fleshed out a coherent theory of how groups develop and carry out their work. Alan Drexler and David Sibbet formulated this model and you can see an informative video on how they derived their model as they worked together.

Here is the YouTube video link:
https://www.youtube.com/watch?v=WA3VkPHp2z0&t=85s

Becoming familiar with the theory and being able to discuss the model easily is critical to delivering this session effectively. As Lewin quipped, "There is nothing so practical as a good theory."

The Drexler Sibbet Team Performance Model can be used to help a team make a quick but powerful assessment of where they are and what they have to resolve on their way to creating and sustaining a high-performance team.

The participants, members of a team, can do a graphical assessment of their team's progress against the 7 Stages and the 21 Keys of the Drexler Sibbet Model.

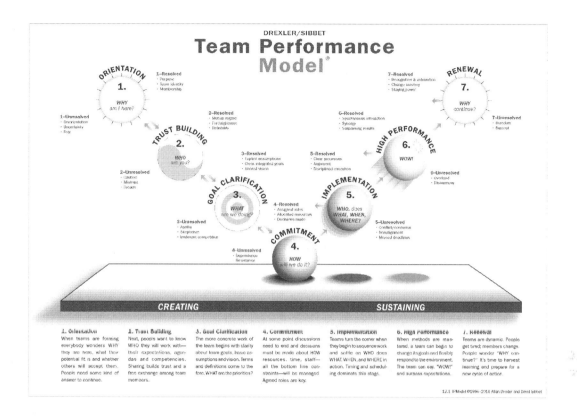

You can order the wall poster and individual model overviews here:
https://grovetools-inc.com/collections/team-improvement

Design and Instructions for the Team Assessment:
- Prior to the session, hang the large Drexler Sibbet Team Performance Model on the wall.
- Make sure it is displayed prominently and in such a way that team members can easily walk up to it and touch it.

- Prepare a short talk on the Drexler Sibbet Model covering the 7 Stages and the 21 Keys. **Note:** The talk should be no longer than 10 minutes. You can tell it as a story about the journey a team takes through time. You should familiarize yourself with the model and become comfortable with the terms.

- Just prior to your talk, hand out the Drexler Sibbet Model Overview to the participants. Ask them to follow along with you.

- Ask the large group to give examples of when they were part of a high performing team. What was it like for them? Ask them to describe their experience using the Drexler Sibbet Team Performance Model. Take several examples.

65

- Ask about our own team. Have people give examples of where they see their current team, using the Drexler Sibbet Team Performance Model.

- Give out red and green Avery dots. Ask the team to go to the large model and place the dots next to the keys they feel are resolved and unresolved. They place green dots on the keys that are most resolved, and red dots on the keys that are most unresolved.

Proud and Sorry
- Write the word "Proud" on one flip chart.

- Write the word "Sorry" on the other flip chart.

- Have the participants make short statements on the flip charts. This can take a bit of time.

- Host an open discussion of what the findings might mean to the group. An effective way to organize this data is to create new charts as follows:
    - **Highlights** - What really stands out?
    - **Concerns** - As consultants: What concerns do you have for this team?
    - **Questions** - Given the data, what are the questions we should be asking ourselves?

- We will illustrate how to do this same design using The Virtual Hive. This will speed up this work exponentially.

Time Involved and Ideal Room Set-up
Total time: Two hours
This design takes about 2 hours to carry out with an intact work team. Use the first thirty minutes to explain the model, how to do the assessment, and the assessment itself. The hour can be used to discuss the findings with the group and to host a Here and Now Session. Use the final thirty minutes to prioritize the findings and to choose what actions to work on together. Following the assessment, you can move to Action Planning.

Materials Needed for this Exercise
- 2 Flip Charts
- Markers
- Red and Green Avery Dots
- Large Wall Chart of the Model
- 1 Individual Model Overview/participant

Contracting and Delivering a Team Off-site

Summary

Contracting with a team leader and with the team is an essential part of the "Action Research" process. Set this up as a role-play where the participants in your class play their roles as accurately as possible. Distinguish between acting and role-playing. Acting follows directions and scenes are fixed according to the script and the director. Role-playing tries to simulate real conditions as much as possible. It allows for participants to try out new behaviors in a supportive atmosphere and provides feedback on their efforts. Role-playing is above all - play.

Design and Instructions for Contracting with Leader and Team

Have participants take turns playing by trying on new roles and trying to adjust their behavior.

Be sure to include separate role-plays for contracting with the team leader and then contracting with the team. The team leader should be asked if it is OK to receive feedback from the team and the facilitator during the session. When contracting with the team and the team leader, do not forget to make use of the Concordant Decision-Making to make the decision to engage in the formal team building intervention.

This design gives the participants a feeling for the contracting process with team leaders and their teams. Contracting is simple, but it is not easy. This design offers the opportunity to "play" with serious issues e.g. leader feedback, team resistance, raising undiscussables, reluctant participants, and so much more. It offers a glimpse into working with a team's group dynamics and how to anticipate different reactions. It is especially helpful for new facilitators to play the different roles in this experience.

Time Involved and Ideal Room Set-up

This design takes two hours.
- The initial set up and role-play take thirty minutes.
- Thirty minutes to contract with the team leader:
- Twenty minutes for role-play and ten minutes for feedback.
- We use the next half hour to cover contracting with the team and the team leader.

The set-up for this is to arrange the chairs in a circle. There is a flip chart off to the side so that the facilitator can scribe important teaching points. The Drexler Sibbet Team Performance Model is displayed prominently. Participants take notes and record their observations.

20. Valentines

Summary

This design is a classic. It was popular years ago as groups struggled with their newly formed matrixed organizations. It is still useful as a way to open up feedback among team members in an intact workgroup or between two or more teams. The exercise itself is simple and direct. It is an enormously powerful intervention because when it is done with all the relevant players present, solutions become instantly available to the very decision makers that want critical issues between and among each other to be resolved. It is yet another creative way to make use of the Action Research methodology.

This design has the potential to change group dynamics quickly. As Burns said, "It's a rare gift the giver gives us, to see ourselves as others see us." Valentines creates windows of opportunity to see how we are seen and then to consider course corrections to help ourselves and our colleagues and teammates to work together more effectively. When teams work together, there is often some intergroup conflict that naturally occurs. This can also happen on larger teams where there are subgroups that have to work well together. The Valentines exercise is a good one to know how to set up and facilitate, since it can recenter the group and provide an outlet for working through issues.

Design and Instructions

- Have the groups count off to make three groups.

- This exercise is styled to be a learning design. When working with real teams you would use actual live data collected either at the meeting or beforehand (survey, observations, interviews etc.). For our purposes, have each team create "pretend data" to use for the exercise.

- Have each team create one list of the things that often occur at work that foster good teamwork and one list of things that prevent teams from working together effectively. These lists should include some descriptions of behaviors and the effects of these behaviors on the overall team. Give them 10 minutes to do this.

- Have the teams exchange lists.

- From the lists, each team creates two stories. One story for each of the other two teams. They make their stories realistic and they illustrate how their work is affected by the actions of the other two teams. (15 minutes)

Note: There is a difference between role-playing and acting. In acting, the actors follow the direction of the director. They act according to the script and do not vary. In our role-playing we strive to make our reactions as real and as lifelike as possible. This increases the likelihood of real learning taking place.

- Have teams create feedback messages to the other teams. These are in the form of notes written on 5x7 cards. They write numerous notes based on their stories and then they exchange the notes. (15 minutes)

- After each team receives its notes, they read them and discuss the feedback. They reach consensus on what the feedback means and if they wrote down anything that is puzzling or needs further clarification. (15 minutes)

- Next, we fishbowl - one team in the center and the other two teams are outside. A spokesperson shares the response to the feedback from the other two teams. (5 minutes)

Time Involved and Ideal Room Set-up
90 Minutes - Teaching this design can go a lot faster than doing it live with an intact team or several teams working together to resolve issues. Leave at least 90 minutes to practice formulating questions, naming the sub-teams, giving the feedback, and responding with action plans and / or course corrections.

Materials Needed for this Exercise
- Flip Charts for each group
- 5X7 Index Cards

21. Two Truths and a Lie

Summary

This is a fun exercise to begin the process of disclosure and feedback. Often people are surprised at the adventures their co-workers have had. They learn together while laughing at the surprises that pop up. This is a useful design to do at dinner or as an afternoon opener. The ideas generated will become great topics for informal conversations. It is a simple and fun way to invite people to loosen up and disclose a bit more about themselves. Each time we give permission to a group to disclose more, we open up the possibility for more feedback as well. Remember the Johari Window is the theoretical framework for this design. The more I open up to you the more likely you will reciprocate. It is a light exercise in disclosure, and it is low risk and fun.

Design and Instructions

- Each person lists three "facts" about themselves, except one of the "facts" is a lie. Be sure to be random about the order of your presented "facts." Also try to recite the facts in the same voice, so you do not give away the lie.

  Examples:
  - "My uncle discovered a new species of beetle and named it after me."
  - "Over seven summers in high school and college, my father and I hiked the entire Appalachian Trail."
  - "Two summers ago, my family took our vacation to Ohio for a family reunion. There were 237 relatives there."

- Don't tell any facts or lies that might make others feel uncomfortable.
- The other people guess which one is a lie. Everyone gets a turn guessing.
- Once everyone is finished guessing, the person sets the record straight by identifying his or her lie. They may also explain the circumstances for the other two facts. Everyone else may talk about how he or she was fooled or how he or she figured out which was the lie.

Time Involved and Ideal Room Set-up

This exercise takes about three minutes a person.

Be careful about the size of the groups. If the group is exceptionally large, have two sessions going. Then have each session nominate their best surprise.

22. The Prisoner's Dilemma

Summary

This exercise illustrates how a contrived situation can affect trust in a group. This is an amazing exercise because it demonstrates dramatically how easily trust can erode when communication is limited and where the stakes appear to be high.

The group will experience what happens when instructions are vague, and the groups are given a potentially highly competitive task to carry out. The aim for the facilitators is to leverage the reactions that occur in the debrief of the exercise to help the group learn about how assumptions affect outcomes. The exercise is particularly effective in illustrating some of the pitfalls and paradoxes that must be addressed and worked in a matrix organization. **Note: It is not intended to be used as a team building exercise. Use this only in the laboratory to illustrate the dynamics that are in play in a Matrix-Environment.**

Background

The Prisoner's Dilemma is an "older" exercise. I first experienced it in the 60s in a group dynamics course. It became overused and ineffectively facilitated during the 70s. It caused lots of pain in working groups and because of this, it fell into disuse. I resurrect it in this course because of the potential for learning. Its origins are from game theory and it is known as a classic zero-sum game.

It is called "the Prisoner's Dilemma" because it sets up the same dynamics that occur when the police capture two suspects and charge them with a murder. They isolate them for a time and then talk to one of them and say, "Look Bugsy, you better confess, we talked to your buddy, Alphonse, and he pointed to you as the trigger man. This means you get the needle, and he gets off for co-operating. So, if you confess, we will go lighter on you. You may actually avoid the needle."

At which point Bugsy says, "You got it wrong man, Alphonse did the shooting, and he's lying! I'll tell you everything!"

Do you get the picture? Do not tell the group this explanation until the debrief!

Design and Instructions

This design always works. All you really have to do is introduce the exercise, give some very strict instructions, and then watch the dynamics. As Yogi Berra said, "You can observe a lot by just watching."

- Divide the group into two groups. Count off.

- Introduce the design by saying you are going to take part in an exercise that simulates the dynamics of a matrix organization.

- Move one group to the other room. Have one facilitator lead them there.

- Give both groups the instructions sheet and the pay-off schedule.

- Tell them to read the instructions to themselves. State that the goal of this game is to earn as many points as you can. Say no more.

- Position yourselves outside of both rooms. Take a flip chart and create a scoring sheet. The sheet will be used at the end of the experience to show the group what happened in each round.

- Decide between the two of you who are facilitating, who will keep score and who will be the runner.

- Play the game.

Debriefing the Exercise

Following the game, assemble both groups auditorium-style and discuss what happened. There will be lots of energy. Facilitate an open discussion. Ask each group to explain their assumptions about how they played the game. Follow the energy. Some questions you might want to ask:
- How did you decide on how to play?
- What were the consequences of your decisions?
- How does this exercise simulate working in a matrix?
- What are you learning?
- Ask about the negotiating rounds
- What happened? Why?

After the very end of the exercise, you can read this to the group:

Back-story

Bugsy and Alphonse have been arrested for robbing the Hibernia Savings Bank and placed in separate isolation cells. Both of them care much more about their personal freedom than about the welfare of their accomplice. A clever prosecutor makes the following offer to each: "You may choose to confess or remain silent. If you confess and your accomplice stays silent, I will drop all charges against you and use your testimony to ensure that your accomplice does serious time. Likewise, if your accomplice confesses while you remain silent, they will go free while you do the time. If you both confess, I get two convictions, but I will see to it that you both get early parole. If you both remain silent, I will have to settle for token sentences on firearms possession charges. If you wish to confess, you must leave a note with the jailer before my return tomorrow morning. The "dilemma" faced by the prisoners here is that, whatever the other does, each is better off confessing than staying silent. But the outcome obtained when both confess is worse for each than the outcome, they would have obtained had both remained silent.

A common view is that the puzzle illustrates a conflict between individual and group rationality. A group whose members pursue rational self-interest may all end up worse off than a group whose members act contrary to rational self-interest. More generally, if the payoffs are not assumed to represent self-interest, a group whose members rationally pursue any goals may all meet less success than if they had not rationally pursued their goals individually.

Puzzles with this structure were devised and discussed by Merrill Flood and Melvin Drescher in 1950, as part of the Rand Corporation's investigations into game theory (which Rand pursued because of possible applications to global nuclear strategy).

The title "Prisoner's Dilemma" and the version with prison sentences as payoffs are due to Albert Tucker, who wanted to make Flood and Drescher's ideas more accessible to an audience of Stanford psychologists. Although Flood and Drescher did not themselves rush to publicize their ideas in external journal articles, the puzzle attracted widespread attention in a variety of disciplines. Christian Donninger reports that "more than a thousand articles" about it were published in the sixties and seventies. A bibliography (Axelrod and D'Ambrosio) of writings between 1988 and 1994 that pertain to Robert Axelrod's research on the subject lists 209 entries. Since then the flow has shown no signs of abating.

Time Involved and Ideal Room Set-up
This design takes two hours.
Do not try to cut the time short. It takes an hour to set up and run the game and then another hour to process the debrief. Ideally set up the "prisoners" in two different rooms so they cannot hear each other. Set up the scoring separately but close to the two rooms. One facilitator manages the scoring and the other is the runner and collects the scores from each of the subgroups in each round.

Materials Needed for this Exercise:
2 Flip Charts
The Instructions and Scoring Sheet for each group

The Instructions and the Scoring Sheet are in the Appendix.

23. Renew and Restore

Summary

This design is to facilitate communication between two team members (executives, co-workers etc.) who are in conflict with one another. This design has worked very well over the years helping many executives renew and or restore their relationships with other executives with whom they have had interpersonal difficulties.

This design can help executives let go of their differences between each other and create the foundation for a renewed partnership based upon mutual trust. Sometimes despite our best efforts and theirs, the executives choose not to do this work and retain the status quo.

Although conflict is normal and natural on teams, chronic conflict between two team members can be distracting, disruptive, and enervating to the entire team. When this happens, the two parties often cannot resolve it themselves and so, an intervention is necessary. This design describes our method for facilitating a dialogue between the two colleagues and for renewing their working relationship and restoring the trust needed for ongoing collaboration.

Design and Instructions

Our design advocates for an outside facilitator (you) to help intervene into this situation and present the dialogue session as a possible solution. You will need to contract impeccably in order to be successful. The contracting can begin, at any level, it must involve all parties and it must be open and transparent to all involved.

The design is based on FIRO theory: Inclusion, Control, and Openness:
Inclusion - All parties must be involved in the planning, the dialogue, and the follow-up.
Control - All parties must have clear choices made available to them throughout this process.
Openness - All parties must agree to share their thoughts and feelings openly.

The Set-Up

Continuous rancor cannot continue on teams. When it occurs between two people there are only four options:
Option 1: Person A leaves the Team and Person B stays.
Option 2: Person B leaves the Team and Person A stays.
Option 3: Both A and B leave the team.
Option 4: Both A and B stay on the team by resolving their differences and learn how to work together.

Contracting

Begin by contracting with the team leader. Lay out the Set Up as outlined above. State that you will help both parties to work for Option 4. Get the leader's permission to present your design to the two team members.

Contract with each of the two team members separately. Present the set-up options. State that working effectively together is the desire of the team leader and the other team members. Ask each leader if he or she would like to invest in improving their relationship with the other team member. They would need to invest a day of their time working with their teammate and you, an outside facilitator, to find the common ground necessary to renew and restore their relationship. If the leader agrees and the two team members agree, move on to the next steps.

Make sure you contract for a meeting at a neutral site. We like to go to a local bed and breakfast with a comfortable sitting room. Plan for a breakfast and a lunch. Early morning is a great time to begin this work.

In separate places have each leader fill out a flip chart - Strengths and Areas for Improvement. Then have them fill out what they believe the other person will identify as their Strengths and Areas for Improvement. We recommend doing it on one sheet of flip chart paper turned to "landscape mode." See the illustration below for how to do this.

List 8 Strengths	What I believe the other will say about me. List both Strengths and Areas for Improvement	List 5 Areas for Improvement

Sample diagram of the flip chart paper

The Dialogue
Once this work is completed, have both leaders join you in a room. Fold the papers so neither person can see any of the work. Have each person open up the eight strengths.
Read through them and discuss. Make sure that they give examples of how they have seen this strength play out.

Then move to Areas for Improvement. Discuss each one in depth and give specific examples. Share both thoughts and feelings.

Then have each one open up the middle window. They will be surprised at how accurate their perceptions of each other are. This awareness softens the discussion about what is possible.

Break for lunch and take a walk after lunch. The purpose of the walk is to talk about how we might begin to bridge our differences. As a facilitator, act as a witness to this work.

After the walk, move to action planning and agreements. Have them each work on what they will do to improve their relationship and then how they will explain today's work to the team. Set a follow up date to review their progress, perhaps have dinner together.

In our experience this design opens up the possibility for a renewed relationship and a restores trust. Have them report back to their leader with their agreements and their plans.

Time Involved and Ideal Room Set-up
Plan for an entire day.
Go off-site for this design to work. A relaxed bed and breakfast nearby is ideal. Many of these places will let you rent their facilities reasonably for this work. Here is an outline to follow:
- A morning session (inclusion, safety, and listening)
- A mid-day walk in nature
- An afternoon planning session (new actions and follow-up)

Materials Needed for this Exercise
- 2 Flip Charts
- Markers

Day Five - Feedback and Close

24. The Design Clinic

Summary

One of the best ways to see how much the participants have learned during the Action Research Facilitation Laboratory is to engage the group in a Design Clinic. We like to save the clinic experience to the last day, just before the "Genie in the Bottle" design.

The design clinic has been a critical part of this workshop since the beginning. Near the end of the sessions we always include an experience where all participants work together to help design a session. We work in small groups and each participant presents an upcoming meeting, or consulting engagement that they would like help designing.
Examples are:
1. New Leader Assimilation
2. Strategic Off-Site
3. Large meeting of the top leaders
4. Team Start-up
5. Team Tune-up
6. Vision, Mission, Strategy, and Alignment Session
7. Organization Diagnosis
8. Team to Team meetings

The possibilities are wide open for participant engagement. Each group self organizes helps each other out and together they create new possibilities for their consulting and facilitation practice.

Design and Instructions

Explain to the group that they will have a chance to collaborate and create some unique designs that they might apply in some of their upcoming work assignments. They can make use of any of the designs learned this week or any of their original designs.

The Prompts

We expect that they will present their designs as a case study using the following prompts: (These prompts can be written on index cards.)
- Define the meeting or project.
- Who is the meeting owner? (With whom do you contract for this work?)
- What is the meeting about?
- Who are coming and how many participants to you expect?
- What are the outcomes?

Divide the group into small groups of 4-5 participants.

Give each small group a copy of the prompts.

Have each participant pick some upcoming work that they would like to work on with the other participants. They will fill in the prompts and present the idea to their small group. The group will choose one project, meeting, or strategic off-site to work on together.

Small Group Assignment
Using what they have learned this week and what they already know, create a meeting design that meets the client's needs and that they can present back to the large group. Examples might be: On-boarding employees, new manager assimilation, strategic off-site, all hands meeting, policy update meeting, etc.

Note: We like to use 5X7 index cards for the prompts and 5X7 sticky notes for capturing the ideas generated by the participants. The sticky notes are useful because they can be sequenced, re-ordered, changed out. The flexibility helps with creating many ways to achieve the meeting goal.

Give the teams 15 minutes to choose the project they want to work on and 30 minutes to create a preliminary design. Have the small groups present their work, as a case study.

Critique his or her work and involve everyone in the feedback. Note: Those new to designing meetings will usually include many more activities than will fit into the time frame for the design. This is normal and expected.

Debriefing the Exercise
Celebrate their work and decide on what it felt like to design collaboratively. What did you learn? How difficult was it for you? How might you use this experience back with your home team?

Time Involved and Ideal Room Set-up
Total Time: 2 hours for this work
- 30 minutes to discuss the application of their work and to identify their consulting challenges
- 45 minutes to design a session
- 45 minutes to present work to be critiqued by all

Materials Needed for this Exercise
- 5X7 Index Cards and 5X7 Sticky Notes
- Flip Charts
- Copies of the Prompts for each Participant

25. Genie in the Bottle

Summary

Everyone loves the name of this design. We like the "playfulness" in the name, and we use this name to subtlety suggest that feedback can be fun. At best, feedback is an acquired taste. It takes practice and good intent to deliver constructive, specific, and descriptive feedback. "Genie" does all of this within a pure Action Research Design:
- The client formulates the questions
- The client chooses who her or she wants to get answers from
- The consultant works on behalf of the client
- The report is published in the form of a dialogue, and it is witnessed to ensure ownership
- The design equalizes risk across the entire group

This design opens up feedback across a team and it always does by creating a supportive and safe place. We have seen many executives change their behavior through this experience. It uses pure Action Research to gather feedback on everyone's performance in our group. It does so in a helpful way and reinforces all the critical skills emphasized in this workshop. Learn this one well, as you will use it often.

The assumption we make about this exercise is that your fellow team members will tell you helpful information about your performance this week that is specific, descriptive, and useful if you ask for it, you are specific about what you want to know, and you are willing to answer their questions about their performance, as well.

Design and Instructions

The two facilitators who lead this exercise are also involved in it. The instructor is not.

- Have the participants prepare for this exercise by writing their name on the top of a large index card. On the card, have them write down three questions that relate to their performance during our time together. Make sure the questions are legible.
  Examples might be:
    - Please identify 3-5 of my strengths as a facilitator that you saw me display this week. Please be specific.
    - What do you think I miss seeing about myself that if I would see would help me to be more effective?
    - How would you assess my potential as a facilitator and what will I need to work on most?

If you get stuck, remember: start, stop, and continue.

- After writing down the questions, turn the card over and write down the name of eight individuals in this group whom you choose to answer these questions.

- Now form small support groups (triads). Take a few minutes to do this.

- Each person now passes his or her card to the person on the right. When all the participants have exchanged their cards, they simply interview the people on the card. They ask the three questions on the reverse of the card and collect the information for the card's owner. **Note:** make sure people take notes.

- It takes an hour to interview eight people. Keep track of time.

- After the interviews, the participants sit in silence and organize their data- Truths, Trends, and Unique Ideas. (20 minutes)

- After the 20 minutes, reconvene. Ask the group members to meet again in their support groups. The person who collected the data gives an oral report back to the owner of the card. No written material is exchanged. The third person acts as a witness. The timeframe is 10 minutes per person.

- Take breaks as needed.

- Reconvene the group to debrief.

Debriefing the Exercise
Your thoughts about this exercise
- Why does it work?
- Where is the structural tension?
- How would you use it?
- Why is it called Genie in a Bottle?
- Other questions?

Time Involved and Ideal Room Set-up
Total Time: 2-2/12 hours for this design
We do not have a formal set up as the participants simply interview each other. Keeping them close by all in one large room will help manage time.

Materials Needed for this Exercise
- 5X7 Index Cards

26. The Yogi Close

Summary

Closings are difficult. They challenge us to finish our work together well. They tell us something about the impact of the workshop and offer an opportunity to create a memory point - something we can use to remember the workshop. Hopefully, a good close will lead us back to our time together, without trivializing it or making it out to be more than it was.

The best closes are simple and direct, humorous, and compelling. They are a tall order. This is one of my favorites. I call it the Yogi Close. Yogi Berra was a brilliant catcher for the New York Yankees. He also was a famous coach for them as well. And he, without knowing it, became a Zen master! His quotes (koans) show that he reached a remarkably high state of enlightenment, whether he knew it or not!

But see for yourself. Feel free to use this to close the workshop or design a better one that fits your team, the meeting, and the situation.

Design and Instructions

- Pass out the Yogi Berra Quotes List.

- Have people peruse it for three minutes, settling on a quote, which accurately describes some aspect of this workshop. It could sum it all up, or it might represent a feeling you had at a certain time during the workshop.

- Someone starts. Wherever they start, we move to the left until each person is heard. They state the quote and why it seems relevant. If they can end with a Yogi quote of their own, so much the better.

- Open the floor for general comments.

See the Appendix for the full list of Yogi quotes.

Appendix and Forms

Johari Window model

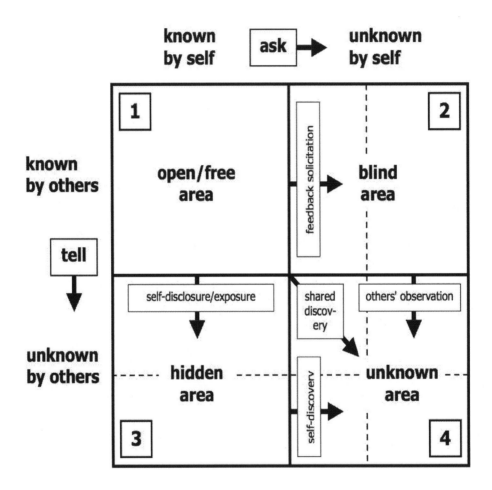

Group Dynamics - Group Observation Form

Leadership (Control - Top / Bottom) Who is leading and who is not?

Membership (Inclusion - In / Out) Who gains, who loses, and how?)

Communication (Open / Closed) Are feelings being disclosed / discussed?

Turning Points (Decision-making) Managing the "groan zone."

Group Dynamics - Who Talks to Whom Form

This is a simple example of a "Who Talks to Whom" Form. Enter the names of the people on the team across in the top column.
Then enter the same names down the first left hand column. Whenever someone talks to someone else, make a hash mark in that box.

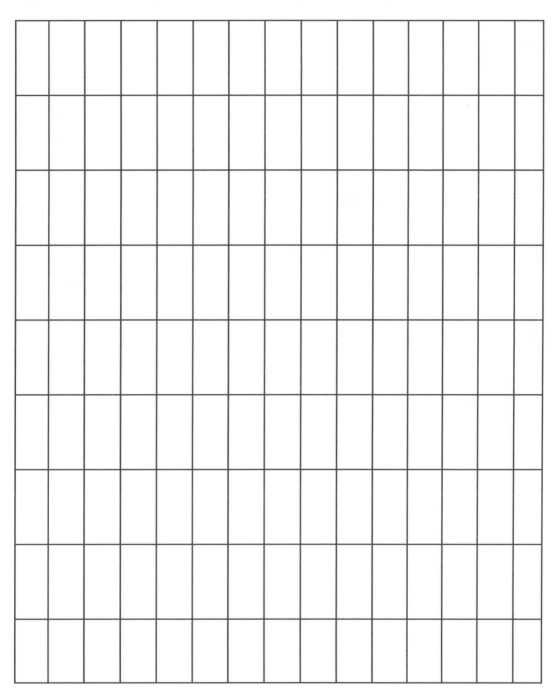

Prisoner's Dilemma - Instruction Sheet

Note: Please read these instructions carefully before you commence play.

Goal: Your goal for this game is to earn as many points as you can.

Play: There are ten rounds to this game. In each round, you will have three minutes in which to select one of three choices: A, B, or C. After each round, a runner will come to your group, take your choice, and then confer with the other runner from the other group. Each group will receive a certain amount of points for the round based on both their choice and the choice of the other group (See below). The runner will inform you of the results after each round.

Scoring: Scoring is cumulative for the ten rounds. Rounds 5, 8, and 10 are Bonus Rounds with higher payoffs.

Negotiation: Before each of the bonus rounds, each group will have three minutes to decide if they wish to send a representative to meet with a representative from the other group, and if so, to give him or her any information needed. If both groups want to have a meeting, they will be so informed, and the representatives will have three minutes in which to negotiate. The representatives will then return to their respective groups, and the decision of the group will be made as usual. This is the only allowed communication between the two groups during the game.

Bonus Rounds Payoffs: For round 5, your payoff points (whether positive or negative) are multiplied by 3; for round 8, multiplied by 5; and for round 10, multiplied by 10.

Prisoner's Dilemma - Payoff Schedule

Your Choice	Their Choice	Your Payoff	Their Payoff
A	A	-2	-2
A	B	2	-2
A	C	4	-4
B	A	-2	2
B	B	0	0
B	C	2	2
C	A	-4	4
C	B	-2	2
C	C	2	2

Yogi Berra Quotes

"I ain't in a slump, I'm just not hitting."

"It ain't over till it's over."

"Baseball's different today, but it isn't."

"If you can't imitate him, don't copy him."

"Are you dead yet?"

"It gets late early out there."

"Ninety percent of this game is half mental."

"When you come to a fork in the road, take it."

"You got to be careful if you don't know where you are going, because you might not get there."

"I really didn't say everything I said."

"Why be jealous over things you don't have?"

"Little league is good because it keeps parents off the street and the kids out of the house."

"Little things are big."

"We made too many wrong mistakes."

"It's so crowded, nobody goes there."

"It was a once in a life time opportunity, and I've had a couple of those."

"If the world were perfect, it wouldn't be."

If you ask me a question I don't know, I'm not going to answer."

"Congratulations! I knew the record would stand until it was broken."

"Someone's got to win, and someone's got to lose, and that was us."

"Pair up in threes."

"The future ain't what it used to be."

"I didn't go crazy over nothing."

"It's Deja Vu all over again."

"You saw Dr. Zhivago? Why, aren't you feeling well?"

"The other teams could make trouble for us if they win."

"He's learning me his experience."

Real-Time Interview Session and Room Set-Up

In Advance:
Have all your flip charts prepared and make sure each seat has the specially prepared notebook/index cards with a pen arranged in the proper sequence. Make sure you have your timer and the sequences ready.

The Flip Charts:
1. **Each question** is written out on separate flip chart page and hung on the wall.

2. **The time sequence** for the major activities is written on a flip chart and posted.
   - 15 minutes - Organize and seat the participants
   - 5 minutes - Introduce the exercise and give instructions
   - 25 minutes - The Real-Time Interviews (each timed sequence is 5 minutes for a total of 25 minutes)
   - 10 minutes - Alone Time to Organize the Data
   - 20 minutes - Group Discussions by Question
   - 30 minutes - Presentation of Truths, Trends and Unique Ideas to the Group (each group has 6 minutes each)

3. **Definition** of Truths, Trends and Unique Ideas is written out and hung on the wall:
   - **Truths** are defined as a statement that everyone you interviewed made. For example, on a given question you interviewed three people and three out of three said the same thing. This is a "truth."
   - **Trends** were not as consistently stated as truths. Only two out of three said it. You declare it a "trend."
   - **Unique Ideas** are just that - one person said it, and you feel it is important for the group to hear, so you declare it a "unique idea."
   -

4. **A separate flip chart** (5) for each of the **question group discussions.** Write the number and each question on the front top of the page. Place the five flip charts into position in advance.

At the Session:
- Greet each person and welcome him or her to your session! This is part of the inclusion phase. Smile and make sure you make eye contact.

- Usher! Funny as this sounds, it is the most important thing you can do to launch Real-Time Interviews well. We like to help them to their seats

- one person stands at the door and greets and the other guides them to their seats. Fill up each set of ten chairs in sequence. When you have ten, move to the next ten. That way you will know if there are any stragglers and whether you have to make some minor changes to the seating.

- Get their complete attention and then begin your instructions. Work from the handout - One person should be guiding the participants through the exercise and another person should be keeping time.

- When the Group Discussion begins, ask each group to appoint a:
  1. **Discussion Leader** - Assures that each person who wants to speak is heard within the time available. Keeps group on track to finish on time.
  2. **Recorder and Digital Recorder** - Writes group's output on flip charts using speakers' words. Ask people to restate long ideas briefly. For large groups you can also request someone to capture the final presentation on a computer.
  3. **Spokesperson** – Select someone to present the data to the group as a whole.

- Upon completion of the RTI Session, thank the participants and tell them what an excellent job that they did. Tell them that a Theme Team will be working this evening to consolidate the overall data for a presentation tomorrow morning.

- **Have them bring all of the five presentations to you and then take them to the Theme Team Room.**

Made in the USA
San Bernardino, CA
01 April 2019